Not Just a Long Walk

Not Just a Long Walk

A Journal of the Camino de Santiago

David Sinclair

Scripture quotations are principally from the Catholic Pastoral Edition of the Christian Community Bible, Fifty-third Edition © 2012 Claretian Publications. All rights reserved.

Cover Design: CFC Youth for Christ UK; remodelled: JP

Copyright © 2020 David Sinclair

All rights reserved.

ISBN: 979-8-64814-669-3

To my mother, whom I miss very much

Those who hope in the Lord
will renew their strength.
They will soar as with eagle's wings;
they will run and not grow weary;
they will walk and never tire.

Isaiah 40:31

Contents

Prologue i

Journal Entries 1

Epilogue 105

Acknowledgements 111

Appendix 1 - Origins of the Camino 113

Appendix 2 - Faith in Action 119

Appendix 3 - Prayerful Findings 123

About the Author 127

Prologue

This is the story of a pilgrim who walked a long mystical path to a very holy site. He set out, like the Magi, not knowing what he would discover and the challenges he would face. He only knew he must go. In prayer, he was asked to share his experiences. I was this pilgrim. This is the journal of my journey.

Why not venture?

If we were to ask a group of people: "Do you dream of pursuing worthy and lofty goals?" most, nearly all, would put up their hand. If then asked: "Do you talk about this aim or do you keep it to yourself?" most, nearly all, would choose one or the other option. If the next question were: "Do you have the determination and willingness to pursue your goal?" how many would still be able to raise their hand to say "yes?"

Too often we can allow what gives us life to be consumed by the circumstances and surroundings that we encounter every day. We remain restless, even lifeless until we tread the path of our vision and follow what genuinely sets us on fire.

In all of this, we know that witnesses are believed because they speak from first-hand experiences, having immersed themselves in their passion. We admire these witnesses who

i

acted boldly and set an example. If we compare ourselves to them, we might say, "I could never do that (it's far too difficult)." We remain cocooned, unable to step through loops of doubt.

With these two thoughts in the backdrop of the quest ahead, let's begin. The scene is set in this Prologue for each day in which God acts through the passage of pilgrims on the Camino.

What is the Camino?

The Camino, which means "walk", "way" or "road" in Spanish, is the pilgrim path to Santiago de Compostela in Northern Spain. It's the Way of St. James. Santiago de Compostela translates as St. James of the Field of the Star. The resting place of the great Apostle. It's a pilgrim path that is now of world renown. Admittedly, there are other spiritual paths and trails, in fact each day is, yet only one Camino.

Appendix 1 gives further information about the origins of the Camino through illustrative modern wall paintings.

Where did it start?

It started in an instant — during the summer of 2018 whilst watching an athletics race on TV I saw the expression of overwhelming joy, the fruit of a lifelong goal, on the face of the winner. I resolved that no matter what sacrifice or hardship, I had to walk the full Camino before returning to my Creator or becoming physically incapable. The pearl of great price (Matthew 13:46) had been found. At this point, I resolved to do everything to preserve the joy of this grace in my heart.

The seed had been planted in earlier years on Caminos of just over 100km in length. These were walked over 4 or 5 days: firstly, on my own; secondly, with my family, and third and

Prologue iii

lastly, with my son. Looking back, the expression on the face of that athlete was the divine instant when it all started.

I asked permission at my workplace for an extended holiday; I never let go of the aim. Strangely, on my desk at work now, I have a mug bought on my last day in Santiago that translates from Spanish to, "The road is the goal — don't let anyone stop you."

Why this journal?

Why make a journal of my Camino journey?

I found the answer in prayer. God wanted me to share this experience. It was God's way of capturing my today for Him. The Camino is predominantly, if not totally, a self-indulgent activity. It is a personal walk. A one-to-one (soul to God), literal and spiritual journey. It was not a selfless Christ-like act of giving.

Yet in prayer, I asked the Lord: How can this be? How can charity be shown?

The reply: "Keep a journal and offer it."

How could I not respond? No matter how tired I might become, I committed myself to recording each day's happenings and discoveries. I had to respond to this task.

The reason my Lord asked me to offer this journal I presumed to be to answer the cry of the poor and indifference toward humanity. That's charity as most understand it to be. All its proceeds go to the charitable work of ANCOP, Caritas and the Missionaries of the Poor (Appendix 2). However, I sense its mission is wider than my initial interpretation as to why. It is exciting to watch its real purpose gradually unfold and become fulfilled.

The Title

Where does the title of this journal, "Not just a long walk" come from?

The title comes from a moment of grace, an inspired moment — a comment that struck me. There could be no other as it would nourish every day of the Camino, and most likely every day thereafter...

Paul Cummins, a good friend from my workplace, held his leaving meal with drinks. I could not miss saying "au revoir." He had recently come into the faith, and on parting that evening he commented on the Camino on which I was about to embark: "Lots of people think it's just a long walk." He lit a torch in an instant to the human reasoning that God can ignite if only we seek Him. Like God's love and embrace itself, some think this is imaginary. The kerygma (the preaching or proclamation of the Christian Gospel) is a mystery some lost souls cannot enter or even allow themselves to be open to as possibly true. It touched the heart of mission, so the comment touched my heart too.

Every day you will find my answer to this question about the Camino at the top of each journal entry — is it just a long walk? In a few words the answer relates to where I was on that day of my pilgrim journey. "It is just a long walk" means I too found the Camino to be just that on that day. Whereas other answers to the question meant the spiritual path and beauty of the Camino were once again evident.

Also, to a degree, this question shaped my reflections and thoughts whilst walking.

My hope and that of my Lord Jesus too, is you shall someday enter a lifelong quest to walk with the living God.

About the Entries

Each day's entry is just that — my thoughts on that day of the Camino — what my Lord presented to me. The entries are the noteworthy snippets. It is written to a degree with an audience in mind, so it is partly personal and partly for sharing.

The exact time logged on Facebook Messenger is also shown in each day's entry unless written late on the next day.

Entries are normally recorded at the city, town or village where I ended up. There are only a few made in transit and they coincidently marked milestones in my progress along the Way.

Most entries have been edited for clarity or to explain the significance of an event, with afterthoughts added to elaborate certain points. Reports of my practical progress are blended with reflections, stories and afterthoughts. Hopefully, items will be palatable, informative, amusing and uplifting. The most contemplative entry is the last and what follows in the Epilogue.

My journal is not a Camino guide and is quite unique.

In its purpose, it is the fruit of an answer to prayer. In its format and style, it is the fruit of a quest for a spiritual path, or dare I say a religious path, along the Way. In its content, I view my experiences through the prism of my Catholic Christian faith. This is a gift with which I have been blessed and is at the root of every reflection I share. I trust they will bridge beliefs and backgrounds.

It's up to every individual to seek God, a great adventure. Once Our Lord is found, there follows an endless relationship to get to know Him and his Mother well. A living relationship.

Lastly, if any comment in my journal offends, this is not

intended. Sometimes we cannot see what someone else holds firm. Please let me know your thoughts so I can learn.

Your Journal

Before moving on, I encourage you to keep a record of your own observations whilst walking the Camino in the blank sections "Notes for My Journal."

Like me, when you return and reflect on these experiences, perhaps you will discover a message the Lord has for you. They may bring a greater meaning to a life in Christ.

My Route

Santiago de Compostela is in the North-West corner of Spain, directly above Portugal.

Take a look at the map of Northern Spain and imagine that the Camino Francés runs parallel to the coast, about 160km inland, from France along almost the whole length of Spain (so from right to left). There you will find the pilgrims' path. It is the most commonly travelled Way. However, for good reason on my route, when I reached Sarria in Galicia I travelled by bus to Ribadeo on the Galician coast, to walk the Camino del Norte for the last 190km to Santiago de Compostela.

The dots on this map trace the places that I stayed at and give a sense of the full route. The names of these places may be gleaned from the heading for each day's journal entry.

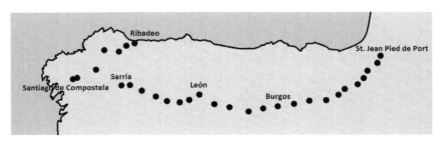

So, at last here it is — my Camino journal. I invite you to read on and be with me along this epic life-changing trail.

Not Just a Long Walk

Journal Entries

These are the places where my day by day journal entries were made:

Preparation Days...3
Day 1 - Stansted, England 5
Day 2 - Roncesvalles, Spain 9
Day 3 - Larrasoaña 15
Day 4 - Pamplona... 17
Day 5 - Puente La Reina.. 21
Day 6 - Luquin 25
Day 7 - Torres del Río 29
Day 8 - Navarrete 33
Day 9 - Santo Domingo de la Calzada 37
Day 10 - Villafranca Montes de Oca 39
Day 11 - Burgos 43
Rest Day 12 - Burgos...45
Day 13 - San Antón 49
Day 14 - Frómista 51

Day 15 - Ledigos 53
Day 16 - El Burgo Ranero 57
Day 17 - León 59
Day 18 - San Martín del Camino 61
Day 19 - Astorga 63
Day 20 - Foncebadón 65
Day 21 - Columbrianos 67
Day 22 - Ambasmestas 71
Day 23 - Triacastela 73
Day 24 - Sarria 77
Recovery Days 25, 26 & 27 - Ribadeo 83
Day 28 - Lourenzá 85
Day 29 - Abadín 87
Day 30 - Miraz 89
Day 31 - Sobrado dos Monxes 93
Day 32 - Monte do Gozo 97
Day 33 - Santiago de Compostela 103

The date and time of each entry is included in its heading along with any contextual information.

Preparation Days

It was during my 2018 Christmas break that I suddenly felt a strong will to walk the pilgrim way from Reading to Southampton. This is in preparation for the full distance (780km) of the Camino Francés.

The Confraternity of St. James had recently updated its guidebook for this pilgrim path, and I remembered I'd bought it. This guidebook is essential — there are no yellow arrows nor waymarkers to follow to the great Apostle's tomb in England! The written directions must be very closely observed to keep on the route and avoid losing one's bearings.

God knew my will. Between January and April 2019, He gave me exactly five days of decent weather on weekends when I had no prior ministry commitments. I escaped during this time to start my fitness trail. My objective was to prepare and revitalise my spirit as I was determined to walk the full Camino — the earthly pearl of great price. With the advice of my chiropractor, Eunjoo Park, I undertook a serious programme of regaining my core body strength through disciplined exercises. Armed with this preparation I could embark with greater confidence.

Along this mini Camino on the morning of Easter Sunday, my final day's walk from Winchester to Southampton, I joined the worship of the Eucharistic celebration at St. Peter's Catholic

Church, Winchester. After Holy Mass I was keen to meet the priest, Fr. Mark Hogan, to let him know I was walking this little travelled Camino route that touches his parish.

Fr. Mark said he had walked the Camino in 1999. He had reflected on what the direction of the arrows meant, yet most markedly he said that the Camino would bring lots of experiences of meeting people along the Way. This comment was made almost as if it ended there — at meeting pilgrims. There's more I thought — it's the Way — otherwise why should I go to extraordinary lengths to secure 40 days and 40 nights to be on the Camino. Prompted by the Holy Spirit, Jesus once did the same — he went into the wilderness to pray, prepare and reflect on his mission; on the reality of his existence in time and space. I know there is much more to the Camino than this, yet the comment stayed.

Southampton Central Railway Station at sunset

I will return to conclude this observation of Fr. Mark's. It is too early to make further comments now — the Camino awaits to provide an answer.

Next is my first journal entry.

Day 1

Stansted, England
flight to Biarritz, France

6 May 2019, 13:13

It's NOT just a long walk

Praise God for He is good. Made it! I'm at Stansted waiting to fly to Biarritz.

I have been as good a servant as I could be, Lord. This morning I met with our blessed new CFC Youth for Christ leaders, Smith and Allyza, and left the YFC UK South mission in their anointed hands. This was after being woken by the Spirit to conclude work for the ANCOP scholars entrusted to the Couples for Christ UK South region.

The remarkable action today...

In 2012 at the Ash Wednesday Mass for the first time ever for Lent, my fast was not to shave for 40 days. Then at the end of that March I walked my 'recce' Camino. I journeyed incognito from Sarria to Santiago with a beard. That stubble has remained ever since — my visible connection to my Lord and God.

Today strangely in the car to the airport, my beautiful wife Vivian and I realized that my electric shaver may not charge up in France and Spain. What could be done? We stopped at the

Services. I shaved off my stubble to be barefaced again. I am young again according to Vivian.

Have I changed over these years of trying to Love?

Lord, as I journey again, please remember that I am bare, with nothing but You as my aid. All my trust is in You now. Afraid a little, yet a young girl, Mary, was once brave and fearless. Today, with that in mind, my theme is "Do not be afraid" ... for my Lord God is with me.

It's about to start!!!

Adrian and I about to set out on the Way in St. Jean Pied de Port

On day 3 of my journal I will introduce Adrian. Needless to say, for now, we met for the first time before take-off!

Explanatory note

Couples for Christ is an international lay community of the Catholic Church. Its focus is the renewal of faith in the family.

Within this community, CFC Youth for Christ and ANCOP are two ministry arms. The vision of CFC Youth for Christ is *young people being and bringing Christ wherever they are* and for ANCOP *bringing Christ's transforming love to the poor.* My role was to locally coordinate this mission.

Notes for My Journal:

Not Just a Long Walk

Day 2

Roncesvalles, Spain
(25 km beyond St. Jean Pied de Port on the Camino Francés)

7 May (recorded 8 May, 17:21)

It IS just a long walk

For most pilgrims St. Jean Pied de Port is the start of the Camino Francés. Yet translated, Pied de Port, means "base of the pass." It's easier for a camel to pass through the eye of a needle than it is to reach the Kingdom of God. So it is to start the Camino, the Way, for a man or woman today setting out on this spiritual path * see the related story.

It is, in fact, the hardest day, with a rating of one to five for every day in the guidebook. It is a five, the only five. Just relentlessly up and up. Yes, relentless. Although then you learn that it is the easiest way that pilgrims could find through the Pyrenees!

Let's think again. Like all paths that lead to God you only need start on the journey and trust. He will make a way and reveal the Way. However, my old friend from France in the first albergue filled me with terror with his daunting description of the ascent to Roncesvalles, and my wonderful hosteller, Marie Stella, did not allay my fears either! Fortunately, both exaggerated.

The reward of the great ascent and sharp 4km descent was staying at the monastery of Roncesvalles (valley of thorns), along with 217 other travellers. Later on, I learnt that 500 started on 1st May and 400 a fortnight later, overwhelming facilities and distressing hostellers. Police opened a hall to cope with this number of pilgrims.

Holy Mass is offered at 8pm with a pilgrim blessing in every language of an incredible number of different nationalities. This is followed by a tour, with explanation in Spanish, of the church, crypt, cloister, and chapel house with a statue of a King of Navarre, Sancho Seventh the Strong. My Spanish is awfully poor, so I struggled to understand anything the priest who had offered the tour, was saying. I had no translator as my friend, Adrian, was not present.

Statue of Our Lady on the first day's climb in the Pyrenees

Finally, rest! My legs will ache all night!

* Related story (on starting out on my first Camino)

My first Camino was from Sarria to Santiago de Compostela on the Camino Francés.

This first Camino was a 'recce' — I wanted to gain a sense and understanding of what it's all about. I intended to walk the whole of the Camino Francés at a later date. This intention fell away on my return. Although by the testament of this journal, in God's time, it came to be.

At that time, I had no reservations about walking the Camino. This outlook of mine seems to be in contrast to many who have walked or cycled the Way.

Some people can spend months or years meticulously preparing or psyching themselves up before they are willing to go. Similarly, some require inordinate details. In this delay, their initial desire to set out is in danger of being lost or forgotten. Sadly, some never get around to it. Others, for many reasons, flatly rule out the possibility. They may be too old, have a health condition or are unable to walk or travel. Alternatively, they may be constrained by dependent family members or unable to afford the expense. Back then, without realising, I fortunately did not fall into any of these categories and just went.

Additionally, I almost went without a Camino guide! I'd been advised that I didn't need one because the pilgrim path is easy to follow. This is true — the route is easy to follow with its many signs, yellow arrows and scallop shells that give directions and point the way to pilgrims.

However, a guide holds important additional

information about the route, namely: what to do, places to stay and sites to visit, with details that would otherwise be missed about towns and their origins. Fortunately, I realised just in time that the advice was overconfidence — it was too much to ask anyone starting out for the first time to go without a guide. I ordered one and fortunately, it arrived the day before I departed. It was only on my flight to Santiago that I was able to learn about some prerequisites for the Camino as I read its 'Before You Go' section!

Thinking back, I was naïve on this recce Camino. I distinctly recall after three days walking, a pilgrim only just managing to decipher my ridiculous pronunciation of 'albergue.' This is the hostel in Spain where most pilgrims stay. It's pronounced, "ahl-behr-geh."

An even more astonishing fact about my rawness was that I didn't know what was meant by, "Buen Camino." A pilgrim said it to me in the dormitory of very first albergue in Portomarin. I was puzzled by the phrase and asked her what it meant. It is the commonly used expression to wish a pilgrim a good journey, especially in passing. I consider the saying to be identical to the Jewish expression, "Shalom", which is also used by Christians. It means both hello and goodbye (suitable as pilgrims pass each other), as well as expressing to the recipient: peace, harmony, wholeness, completeness, prosperity, welfare, and tranquillity. Quite a lot of good wishes packed into a word, or into the two Spanish words, "Buen Camino."

I left for this first Camino on 26th March 2012. This was the start of British Summer Time. With the clocks moving forward by an hour I was given long days of

Day 2 – Roncesvalles, Spain

light to walk in. On my first day, not only did I fly from Stansted to Santiago, travel by bus to Lugo then Sarria, source a pilgrim's passport known as a 'credencial' (this is a story I return to later), I also savoured every minute of the walk to Portomarin — the first stage in my new guide book. I arrived in Portomarin at dusk and by the time I had found my albergue, it was dark.

Glorious sunny days followed; I was given the most blessed week. My Lord shone brightly throughout in every way.

Notes for My Journal:

Not Just a Long Walk

Day 3

Larrasoaña
(5.3km beyond Zubiri)

8 May, 18:40

It IS just a long walk

I am starting to ask myself — where is the spiritual path? It's the busiest time for this stage of the Camino and nearly everyone is a walker, not a pilgrim.

God gave me Adrian Croft, a retired Reuters reporter. We met literally on the flight. We sat side by side in the aisle and conversed all flight about the Camino.

My concern about whether I would get to St. Jean Pied de Port on the first day went away thanks to Adrian. I had silently been presenting this to my Lord. With a rushed email a minute before take-off to join his communal taxi (a pilgrim service direct to St. Jean Pied de Port, €19). On arrival I received a confirmation reply and found I had the last space of eight! How amazing and good is God? Luke, though, on the same flight and with whom I 'dormed' next to on the next day in Roncesvalles, still managed to get a bus from Biarritz to catch the only train at 6:30pm from Bayonne.

Adrian has been a guardian angel and I am thankful. We meet tomorrow at 8am to walk together to Pamplona.

Stop press! As I write this from my albergue, I meet TJ from the USA, a genuine pilgrim at last. A man that is very much in need of the Camino, as strongly suggested by his priest, for what I pray will give clear guiding light to his next phase of life.

I gave TJ my first St. James Cross lapel pin in the hope that this tiny gift would leave a heartfelt lasting memory. On my last Camino with my son I bought 12 of these distinctive pins in Santiago de Compostela to give, as someone once gave to me on my first Camino, to pilgrims that God puts in my path.

Notes for My Journal:

Day 4

Pamplona

9 May, 18:42

It's NOT just a long walk

I'm writing from the municipal albergue in Pamplona of Jesus y Maria, part of a former Jesuit church, sleeping on the top bunk of 30+ cubicles built into the naves — that sounds great, yet it could be cold tonight with the tall ceiling and glass walkways above.

Today I will reflect on my walking companions ... they are the most reliable pair, always steady on my journey, giving power when I'm weak and need strength. I'm able to rest on them. They are a source of real companionship and there's no way that I could complete the Way without them. Strangely one was injured today, and I reacted quickly enough to save him, just, thank God.

My companions' names are James and John. They are my walking sticks — I do cherish them. They were bought on arrival in St. Jean Pied de Port in the Camino shop on Rue de la Citadelle (www.boutique-du-pelerin.com). This shop can be found on the route of the Way near the Pilgrims' Office, where I obtained the first stamp in my credencial, shown here.

Now at every stop as you leave, the tip is to count the items you carry — I have four: backpack, day bag, and James and John, whom I nearly left behind (on my second day a young Korean walker actually left his crafted wooden walking stick). My own sticks are bamboo with metal pointed spikes, which should be flattened by the end of my Camino walk, and are about 5ft tall. I hurt one by catching the tip in a bridge gap and it cracked the glue and nearly snapped off. Although they nurse me along, I too must care for them. I hope that James, who's damaged, makes it to Santiago.

*Strengthened by James and John
- my bamboo walking sticks*

Pamplona is famous for its fiesta when bulls stampede through its narrow streets chasing boys who want to prove their manhood. Every few years someone dies. Animal rights protesters give entertainment too by running through these

Day 4 - Pamplona   19

streets naked before this festive tourist draw starts. Otherwise, by day, Pamplona is a calm and quiet city, with its university student population bringing it to life by night.

I spent some time with Scott who I had earlier met on the Way. He is a bee-keeping Australian who comes from 300km outside Adelaide, and a fount of information, having already walked the Camino Francés. We shared the cost of a laundry in the nearby launderette and a delicious meal of fresh brown bread with sliced tomato in the courtyard of our Jesus y Maria albergue.

Notes for My Journal:

Not Just a Long Walk

Day 5

Puente La Reina

10 May (recorded *11 May, 20:26*)

It IS just a long walk

At the highest point of the climb today, there is a spot where a scene from the Martin Sheen film "The Way" was shot. An inscription describes the set of sculptures that represent the evolution of the Pilgrims' Way as, "Where the route of the wind crosses that of the stars." With the wind turbines in the area this inscription aptly describes the location, yet from a Camino perspective, you could translate it to where the spirit meets the pilgrim, or where man meets himself. The insight seems to have captured the quest of most who journey on the Camino for their spirit.

My desire to be close to my Lord increases. At this point I am still seeking that intimacy. Even on the Camino it is not quiet, especially now as its popularity is so great. Perhaps on past Caminos I was spoilt or blessed. Most souls that are walking are trying to figure things out, and slowly are. I trust you, Lord, if this is what you want for me, please satiate my desire to be with You.

The mixture of cultures and nationalities on the Camino is vast. In practical terms the Way is physically tough on the body. Adrian and I are still together, conversing continually.

My message from this period is that it's not an even and perfect way, but just like every avenue of life, it's made smooth by grace!

The place where St. James first preached in Padrón

Afterthoughts (on prejudice)

On the Camino Portugués, Padrón is the town where St. James first preached the Gospel to the Iberian people. Upon my arrival in Padrón with my son, Andrew, in May 2018 I immediately visited the actual place of his preaching.

Whilst on my way down from this place, a Dutch pilgrim asked me, "Which is the more important — Padrón or Santiago de Compostela?" I wanted to answer Padrón, even though it is a quiet and scarcely visited place. However, my answer must be both. Padrón because Christians live for the proclamation of the Good News and Christ's return. Yet on the road to Santiago an awakening can happen. Along the road souls are open to be touched by God. Therefore, the great Apostle is in a way still preaching from his tomb, as St. Francis of Assisi said, "Preach the Gospel at all times and when necessary use words." Therefore, Santiago de Compostela is equally as important because it continues to draw many souls to listen to Saint James and begin to understand his mission.

I add this story as an afterthought because a lesson is given on the Camino where a diverse multitude of languages, ethnicities, cultures and beliefs come together. This lesson is to "get off your high horse" by accepting pilgrims as they are; not judging, in any way, how they make their journey. They have all been given a means and desire to be on this transforming Camino path. It is not by coincidence that God places them there. I must always remember to be grateful and respectful to every person placed in my path.

Notes for My Journal:

Day 6

Luquin
(11.6km beyond Estella)

11 May, 20:26

It IS just a long walk

Ancient Chinese philosopher Lao-tzu said, "To attain wisdom, remove things every day." Certainly, my backpack is heavy! I learnt today that I can send items on by post to Santiago to pick up on arrival. For sure my small bible needs to go ahead.

Today I walked on past Estella, the next town that my Camino guidebook suggests stopping at, and left Adrian there in his pre-booked accommodation. This meant there was a little time to reflect.

By the way, God is so good that when I got to my destination and discovered that the albergue where I intended to stay was full, He had it covered. Before needing to walk on for another 12km to the next accommodation, the hosteller of an albergue on the alternative Camino route literally arrived at that exact moment and drove me to his albergue. What timing Lord!

The reflection is on respect. One of my brothers in Christ I can picture saying — respect is the greatest virtue or character gift, affirmed fully by the title Reverend Father (Rev. Fr.). This is the respect given in title to a holy man, ordained to minister to Our Lord's people. To counter this, respect is earned, not demanded or expected by status or position.

When Filipinos meet, the young immediately show respect to their elders by taking the hand of the elder and raising it to touch their forehead whilst simultaneously lowering their head to meet the elder's hand. They also address elders with the word "po." Is this genuine respect or just custom? * also see the related story.

When we enter a church, do we genuflect (kneel on one knee) and affirm out of great reverence, "My Lord and my God" (John 20:28) as we face the Blessed Sacrament in the tabernacle? Or do we just half genuflect out of routine and because everybody else does it?

How do you overcome the struggle to respect who you must, even though they demonstrate no humility or compassion? Those with set ways and closed minds, or who 'categorise' a person. Those who never say, "sorry." Showing respect to these people is only possible with the strength and with the grace of the Holy Spirit. If voices are raised, then respect is lost and no good can come. Once lost, respect can be restored by great love and reconciliation by all.

* Related story (on the worldwide popularity of the Camino and my Filipino connections)

This next story is an example of the incredible number of countries that the Camino has reached, and is reaching today, with the faith it brings and awakens in individuals and groups. Apart from illustrating this growing widespread popularity of the Camino that draws pilgrims from all over the world, it also helps explain my deep love and bond with everybody and everything Filipino. It's why there are several references in my journal to the Philippines and two of the three charitable projects it supports are based there.

Early one morning during Semana Santa (Holy Week) in March 2018 I rose to join a procession through the streets of Compostela, Cebu, Philippines. As I strolled to the Church of St. James the Apostle, I prayed the rosary. Whilst waiting for the procession to start outside the church I was asked if I would kindly meet the parish priest. Fr. Deligero Scipio had noticed me with my rosary in my hand and wanted to meet. It was a sight that must have stood out to him as it's highly unusual to see a foreigner on his own deep in prayer.

I obviously agreed and walked over to the church entrance, where Fr. Scipio was sitting, to meet him. After a greeting, he immediately asked, "Do you know about the Camino?" "Yes Father, I have walked the Camino twice and very much love it." I was amazed by this question and wondered how he knew me.

This thought was triggered because when Vivian and I were married in the same church, the priest who administered the Sacrament of Holy Matrimony, knew by the advice he gave in his homily the main weakness of our characters, even though he didn't know us. So, I was beginning to think that all Filipino priests at her ancestral parish were divinely psychic!

In our meeting Fr. Scipio fondly spoke about the Camino and how much he longingly hoped to walk it in Spain, although his body was starting to fail him. We were now instant friends. He had inspired me to walk it again and our meeting was another reason why shortly after returning from our holiday, I opportunely walked the Camino Portugués with my son.

I learnt afterwards that Fr. Scipio and his parish were to host the next annual National (Philippines) Congress of Santiago de Compostela Parishes and Devotees on 5-6th February 2019. I also learnt that a Camino route had been established across the centre of the island of Cebu, from St. James the Apostle Church in Badian to St. James the Apostle Church in Compostela. This is one that I hope to walk someday.

Lastly, I learnt that for this Congress a large image of the Botafumeiro had been erected outside the church. The Botafumeiro (Galician for "smoke expeller") is the famous huge thurible that is swung by rope across the Santiago de Compostela Cathedral during Holy Mass to incense the altar and thereby lift the prayers of the faithful to God. In times of plague, it was thought to also have an actual cleansing effect on the pilgrims, as well as a spiritual one.

Day 7

Torres del Río

12 May, 14:26

It's NOT just a long walk

A beautiful night in Torres del Río

I only walked 19km today so that Adrian and I can meet up in Torres del Río on the border of the Basque Country. Unfortunately owing to lack of information and my arrival time in towns I missed Sunday Mass. My wife, Vivian, messengered prayers of spiritual communion to atone.

Today whilst walking, praise God, the Way started to open. I encountered open green fields with shafts of corn like long grass and a blue sky, sun and all sorts of small birds, a dawn chorus, peace, quiet, idyllic and picturesque towns. Thank God that the Way exists and if you can open the eyes of your heart you can see the beauty it offers the souls on pilgrimage.

I reflected on why I personally love the Camino so much and why others do. Many, after walking it, return to offer services to other pilgrims because they want to give back what the Camino gave them. A Dutch couple operating a mobile camper van to give away drinks, snacks and fruit for donations is just one example.

The Camino is where I connected with God on my recce Camino in 2012. Why would I not want to return to that place? I have tried other pilgrimages. Yet never since has the connection been as close as on that first solo Camino. This is also in spite of serving tirelessly and without ceasing Our Lord's people, with all my strength and my mind. However, I had the audacity to presume that because I sacrifice and meditate for 40 days and 40 nights I would connect again. This time in a greater way. Forgive me, Lord, that I would dare to know your plans, for my thoughts and ways can never know yours. Whatever your Will for me during this small time on your Way, let me accept it with a humble heart.

Moving back to the fields, I was led to the scene in the Gospels where the Pharisees challenge why Jesus' disciples picked heads of corn to eat on the Sabbath which was against the Law of Moses (Matthew 12:1-8). It is how I could picture this scene, yet in reality it was possibly quite different, and the evangelists were poetic in writing. Maybe it's why I was not led to Mass, for "The Sabbath was made for man, not man for the Sabbath." Jesus had led me there already in a sense in the fields of the Way, knowing He is the bread of life, the eternal sacrifice so that we may be with Him in our today, He is Lord of the

Sabbath. This thought is all my poor soul needed to sustain my life in Him. God is amazing.

Worn everywhere for over four months to break them in ready for the Camino - my perfect walking shoes

---

Notes for My Journal:

Not Just a Long Walk

Day 8

Navarrete

13 May (recorded 14 May, 18:47)

It IS just a long walk

We walked 32km today and all around Logroño. This resulted in the first appearance of blisters!

Some useful practical advice for future pilgrims: In Logroño I dropped off 2.75kg of excess items to be picked up at the Santiago main Correos (post office) using a service called 'Peregrino Pac' that allows pilgrims to send on items. This service cost me €32 for 30 days' storage plus box, or it's around half this amount for 15 days, with every extra day incurring a €1 charge. My backpack is lighter now, alleluia.

Pretty boring route! Shall I remember this day as the day of the supermercado? We spent ages looking for a supermarket that stocked only basic items, only to proceed to walk by 3 big supermarkets on the long walk out of Logroño!

Then, God lifts everything, we arrive at our centrally located albergue and meet Delia, the hosteller, from Zaragoza. She's a bubbly great character, full of life. We check in, and I get a special bed.

A little while later, Adrian returns from the supermercado and says to me in a bar. "You've got to go to the church now. It's just around the corner." As I walk in Adoration is finishing and is followed by Holy Mass. I wonder whether I should receive Communion, having drunk a beer 20 minutes before the start of Mass. I conclude that I was innocent to the need for the Eucharistic fast and Our Lord would want to be close. He would forgive my ignorance of the imminent Mass.

After Mass, all pilgrims received a blessing and I joined the procession, following a statue of the Virgin Mary around the church with a lighted candle, given to me by Delia. Following this, the priest invited pilgrims to the sacristy with great Catholic treasures and holy paintings. Delia then embraced Adrian and me in the bar. We had paella and exchanged contacts.

Fresco from the sacristy in Navarrete

The next day, at the reception of the albergue, she had left a note for Adrian, and had given him a ribbon from Our Lady of the Pillar, for protection on his journey. Like the scallop shell of St. James, one of these ribbons is tied to my backpack, so I was pleased. For the pilgrim this ribbon represents the mantle of healing and protection that surrounds the pillar in Zaragoza

Day 8 - Navarrete

on which the Virgin Mary appeared to St. James. I pray that Adrian will come to fully understand Our Lady's maternal love for him. Our Lord's people are amazing!

Notes for My Journal:

Day 9

Santo Domingo de la Calzada

14 May (recorded 15 May, 18:39)

It IS just a long walk

Adrian and I parted after 15km at Nájera. He wanted to learn about the Kings and Kingdom of Navarre at the Monastery of Santa María la Real de Nájera. Nájera to Santo Domingo de la Calzada is the most beautiful walk. Despite starting late in the morning, the path is inviting, and I was able to enjoy the endless fields whilst ambling along praying and meditating on the rosary for the first time on the Camino. Time drifted and I found myself in Santo Domingo at 4:30pm.

The glory of the Meseta — reflective beauty and peace to remain in

I am staying at the albergue Abadía Cisterciense, supposedly run by nuns. It's a peaceful and relaxing old place, with the tiny downside of a poorly strung bed! The thought of staying here is what drove me on during the day and it was worth it.

Not Just a Long Walk

Coincidentally it is also the fiesta celebration of Santo Domingo, held over the first two weeks of May. At the end of Holy Mass, we, the faithful, were able to venerate his relic. The next day I will pass by his place of birth on the Way.

Saint Domingo de la Calzada dedicated his life to improving the Way for pilgrims in the 11th century. Amongst other pursuits, he built roads for pilgrims, called calzada. The town is in a festive mood with singing, dancing and a food offering to the hundreds of townspeople going on till late.

Adrian managed to keep walking to my dorm too, but we parted the next morning to walk alone. Not sure if we will meet up again! It has been great travelling with him. Thank God for such friends.

Notes for My Journal:

Day 10

Villafranca Montes de Oca

15 May, 18:39

It IS just a long walk

Not the best day. I walked about 36km, and a long way in the heat with a heavy backpack owing to food and water supplies added in Belorado. My knee hurts and I am unsure about making tomorrow's destination — a long walk to Burgos, which is a huge city with a population of 180,000 and it's a long way through the suburbs into the centre.

The scripture opposite relates to a reason for this journal — the ANCOP Cornerstone project — to help young slow readers in the Philippines. I knew this verse would be in this journal when I prayed the words.

Morning Prayer

Short Reading   **Ephesians 2:19-22**

In Christ you are no longer aliens, but citizens like us

You are no longer aliens or foreign visitors: you are citizens like all the saints, and part of God's household. You are part of a building that has the apostles and prophets for its foundations, and Christ Jesus himself for its main cornerstone. As every structure is aligned on him, all grow into one holy temple in the Lord; and you too, in him, are being built into a house where God lives, in the Spirit.

Prayed whilst walking
© 1996-2019 Universalis Publishing
Ltd. (mobile app.)

Also included in Appendix 3 are four beautiful pilgrim reflections and prayers that I received along the Way.

As I walked earlier today, I read and pondered on St. James' scenes in the Gospels.

He was called by Jesus, with his brother John, on the shore of the Lake of Galilee. At once they left to go with Him (in Matthew and Mark's Gospel account). Naively I thought this was instantaneous. Yet, the seed must already have been planted in his heart. Jesus and the brothers may have conversed for a while and James, as a good Jew, was waiting for a Messiah. As a group, with Simon Peter, Andrew and John, it must have been easier to respond to Jesus' calling, encouraged by each other. This first encounter though in some ways for St. James was his kerygma — the birth of his following.

Since returning I learnt that John, the brother of James, had already spent several hours with Jesus (John 1:35-42) before they met on the shore of the Lake of Galilee. In his Gospel account, John referred to himself in the third person. Therefore, it's likely that he was the other disciple of John the Baptist that went with Andrew to follow and stay with Jesus when John the Baptist said, "There is the Lamb of God." Like Andrew, afterwards, he too would have told his brother James about the Messiah. This would have made it easier for the brothers to recognise Jesus and to leave their father Zebedee when Jesus summoned them (Matthew 4:21-22).

Yet Luke gives a different Gospel account. One in which it is easier to understand why, "leaving everything", James would instantly follow Jesus. Here we have the supernatural catch of two boats full of fish "to the point of sinking." Jesus had asked Simon Peter for faith, "Put out into the deep" and "Simon's partners, James and John" were amazed at the resultant catch. They were skilled fishermen who knew the waters and had "worked hard all night and caught nothing." Only they would realise this miraculous sign after Jesus' teachings to the crowd

Day 10 - Villafranca Montes de Oca 41

from their boats. He had also remarkably, once again with his new disciples present, provided an abundance of food to those gathered to listen "to the word of God." (Luke 5:1-11)

I'm very tired and need rest, so maybe I'll finish my reflections on the other scenes with St. James on another day.

Notes for My Journal:

Not Just a Long Walk

Day 11

Burgos

16 May (recorded 17 May, 13:38)

It IS just a long walk

I made it to Burgos. God is great — my body held out, although I have a few blisters! Walked 39km from 6:15am to 2:45pm.

I'm staying at the municipal albergue near the cathedral. For my rest day tomorrow, I hope to transfer at noon to a religious albergue (Divina Pastora).

Sunrise at the crest of the climb up Montes de Oca

My first sunrise on the Camino after the ascent from Villafranca Montes de Oca was followed by the calm of the forest.

John's metal spike tip broke off in the forest, so he's now bandaged up, along with James, my other walking stick. At the high point of Alto de la Pedraja, there is a poignant monument to the 300 people that were executed in these mountains by Franco supporters during the 1936-39 Civil War.

For a long time in the morning I dwelt on my ministries in Couples for Christ, how I am perceived and the culture of the community — the path became clear.

Also, whilst on the Way, in a remote countryside area, there was a man standing in the sun, in the open, beckoning every pilgrim to give him a little something. He maybe had to wait between 10-15 minutes for each walker to pass. It was a very unusual scene — never have I seen this before nor after — this solitary figure soliciting alms from pilgrims in the rural terrain of the Camino. May God bless him.

Burgos cathedral at dawn

I finished the day at Adoration and Holy Mass in a side chapel in the magnificent Burgos Cathedral.

Rest Day 12

Burgos

17 May, 16:32

It's NOT a walk

Burgos, Burgos, Burgos. Rest day or not? After such a great day yesterday, all I want to do is walk and pray!

I was not permitted to stay at the Divina Pastora albergue because overnight I ceased to be a travelled pilgrim that needed rest and became a "tourist." Only pilgrims — ones that arrive in a city or town on that day — can stay at municipal albergues unless there is space at 5pm (and that's unlikely). So, I am now staying at a private accommodation, Hostel Burgos, at the huge expense of €17, although this includes breakfast at 6:30am.

I bumped into Alfred from the States, who I'd conversed with on the Camino days earlier, at breakfast in a café on the plaza beside Burgos Cathedral. After this, I went on the audio tour of the impressive cathedral that incorporates the resting place of revered mercenary El Cid.

Chocolate con churros

Not Just a Long Walk 46

Just had my first chocolate con churros — yes, God is good!

I sorted out all that I can and arranged to meet Adrian at 7:45pm after rosary and Mass. My body and feet have not had much time to recover; the day has been far from the restful study day that I'd planned — always on the move!!!

These are recommendations from my Camino friend, Alfred, as we conversed over breakfast:

- Film to watch: 'Capernaum', best foreign language film nomination at the 2018 Oscars
- Spanish song about the Camino: 'Caminante no hay Camino', artist - Joan Manuel Serrat

The title of the recommended song references this well-known poem about the Camino.

Caminante no hay Camino, "Wayfarer, there is no path"
by Antonio Machado, after translation

> Wayfarer, your footsteps are
> the road, and nothing more;
> Wayfarer, there is no road,
> the road is made by walking,
> By walking one makes the road,
> and upon glancing behind,
> ones sees the path
> that will never be trod again.
> Wayfarer, there is no road,
> Only wakes upon the sea.

At the end of this day after Holy Mass in the Capilla de la Divina Pastora, the priest invited the pilgrims who were present to read a Pilgrim Blessing at the altar. The four pilgrims present read the blessing in the four languages on the prayer card: Spanish, German, English, and French. Some of the most commonly spoken languages in the world had a representative. In a sense, all nations of the Lord were there and were blessed.

Rest Day 12 - Burgos

Afterthoughts (on blisters)

It was in Burgos that I decided to pierce a big blister to relieve the fluid. I bought needles and was about to burst it when in my hostel a big South African man with an Afrikaans accent advised, "You don't want to do that. It can lead to infection. The blister is sealed, let it be; let it burst of its own accord." We discussed. He saved me — the next day I met a lady who had spent five days recovering before she could start walking again from an infected blister that she had burst with a sterilised needle.

My South African friend parted by saying, "The Camino is not for sissies!" An unforgettable remark.

The Christian life requires a toughness and resolve to persevere and endure temporary hardships and rejection. Pilgrims must endure Camino blisters! Later I learnt how to care for a naturally burst blister that weeps.

Notes for My Journal:

Not Just a Long Walk

Day 13

San Antón
(5.6km beyond Hontanas)

18 May (recorded 19 May, 07:09)

It's FAR FROM just a long walk

I walked for a long way, beyond where most would stop, because the weather was cool. Actually, it was windy with a chill, and I am now at San Antón, a tiny place. I am staying in an albergue run by an Italian hosteller, Monee. It's inside the ruins of a monastery that has been reopened centuries later, with no electricity, communal everything and obviously cold showers — fortunately, I was not hot or sweaty! It's quite amazing and only accepts donations (is "donativo").

The monastic order of the Hospital Brothers of St. Anthony ran this hospital (refuge) for pilgrims in the 12th century to treat some contagious diseases, especially the so-called "St. Anthony's fire." The Tau Cross of the order, which is blue, is evident everywhere.

God is good as this decision to try this magical place to stay only came after praying the rosary. For this, I craved quiet and had just that bar a few cyclists. This was followed by praying the Chaplet of Divine Mercy, which I finished as I arrived at the magnificent arches of the monastery that form a tunnel over the road of the Way. It was these arches that caused my inquisitive deviation into the jaw-dropping grounds.

I liken this moment at my first sight of the grounds, to the scene in the film, "The Beach" when backpacker, Leonardo DiCaprio, first sets his eyes on the beach. He and his two travelling companions just stopped in awe to take in the unspoilt natural paradise they had sought in front of them.

Thank you, Lord.

Monee in the grounds of the derelict monastery that now houses the albergue that she runs during the warmer months

Day 14

Frómista

19 May, 17:59

It's NOT just a long walk

Apparently, the whole Camino Francés is divided as follows: the first part is physical, the second is spiritual and the third psychological, it's when the mind is working out what to do next.

Certainly, I'm in love with the Meseta, this high (900m average altitude) flat stretch across the Castilla y Leon province. Long paths through fields with nothing but time to pray and reflect. Some don't like it, yet they may have covered the region in the hot season. My days so far have been mild and inviting. It's the reason to take the time to spend time with my Lord.

God held me back today. A late start at 8am after communal breakfast with a most wonderful group of souls, a dog and Monee, the hosteller. A stop to change attire was blessed and necessary, so as I approach the second town (Itero de la Vega) at 11:50am I noticed a local person leave his house and immediately thought — he's going to Mass. He understood "Misa" and my gestures so led me to the local church. Literally just after I had genuflected and sat down, Sunday Mass started. God provided and had his purpose in steering a slow course for me.

Later, unusually and pleasantly, the walk from Boadilla del Camino to Frómista is along a canal. I enjoyed observing the fish in the still water along this stretch. After 29km I decided not to push on as it was 4pm so stopped at the municipal albergue in Frómista.

Approaching Castrojeriz after San Antón on the Meseta

The distant Alto de Mostelares is remarkably similar in shape to Mount Tabor in the Holy Land, the site of the transfiguration of Jesus.

My body is now adapting to the demands of walking a long time carrying my backpack; only my feet don't like it. Patched up John, my walking stick, with a few plasters. God is amazingly good!

Day 15

Ledigos
(3.4km before Terradillos de los Templarios)

20 May (recorded 21 May, 14:02)

It IS just a long walk

Frómista to Carrión de los Condes is just a long walk alongside a track that follows a national road, only deviating slightly at the odd village. The main point of interest along it is Villalcázar de Sirga, which hosts the magnificent Templar church of Santa María la Blanca. The Camino unusually did not pass the church and I arrived too early to detour off as it opens at 10am. Still, the 19km stage only kept me walking from 7am to 10:30am. As it is morning, we are fresh, especially after a massive pastry for breakfast.

The next stretch is the longest ever in a continuous uninterrupted straight line on a flat path, about 15km. It became a physical test of endurance. With James and John giving extra legs nobody passed me as I walked this unique stretch. I pressed on for another 5km on an uneven path and ended up walking over 40km, finishing at 4pm.

Everyone now does the Camino! Today I saw a group of

bikers (Hells Angels) from Germany biking it. There are lots of cyclists in groups from Spain and South America, mainly Brazil. Lots proudly display the flag of their country. The majority of walkers are from: Australia, America, France, Germany, Italy, and Spain. I also met quite a few Brits from all over the UK.

Most people do not like the numbers of walkers. In the morning there are loads on the Way. It's why I like continuing into the afternoon because then it's just me, God and the Way. Yet it's hot and my feet are tired. The best time though.

I learnt the CFC Youth for Christ Liveloud song 'God in me' as I walked. Really uplifting lyrics; a true worship song. Other days were filled by the words of: 'All for You', 'Pour and Flow' and 'In Your Arms.'

I pondered over walking. Every step is one toward a goal — on the Camino it's geographically the great Apostle's resting place. The scallop shell is synonymous with St. James and thereby the Camino. If you look at one, you'll notice that all its ridges lead to the same end — towards God. This is maybe another reason why the scallop shell is used for baptisms — the spiritual birth of a child to God the Father.

Waymarker underfoot

Surprisingly, a few walkers travel in the opposite direction on the Camino. They walk back to where they started * see afterthoughts on pilgrims walking backwards!

Definite goals that are oriented toward Our Lord are all we need for a purpose that fills our hearts with untold joy. This joy gives us super powerful energy and wonderful purpose. Such things surely please Our Lord.

* Afterthoughts (on pilgrims walking back to where they started)

Initially, I laughed at why someone would walk the wrong way! My light-hearted remark, "you're going the wrong way", to a pilgrim walking in the opposite direction caused me to sense that he was greatly annoyed. He must have been tired of hearing this and given up bothering to reply. I refrained after that, and instead made a point of wishing them, "Buen Camino."

Now I greatly admire the additional strength of character they must have to return to the source from which they came. They do not travel with others so have no sustained companionship that is found in fellow pilgrims. The Camino route too must be difficult to follow against the tide of pilgrims.

Also, consider that Jesus had to return to the Father to accomplish his purpose and free all of us who believe in him from captivity. Jesus said, "Abba, Father, all things are possible for you. Take this cup away from me. Yet, not what I want, but what you want." (Mark 14:36). The undying sacrifice of Divine Mercy is evident for the world to see.

In spiritual terms, it is like coming down from the mountain where God is (the pilgrimage destination) to the level of real-life (at the start or one's hometown). I wonder: in which place is life found?

Undeniably to return to the source requires faith, trust and grace. It could be seen as an intent of bringing God's presence back into the everyday mission of life. This is ultimately to be counted amongst the apostles of today, the living saints.

Notes for My Journal:

Day 16

El Burgo Ranero

21 May, 19:43

It IS just a long walk

Again, walking on, 33km, in a straight line along a tree-lined route. The minimal shade that the small trees give is welcome as it is tiring in the heat. I am hoping to press on to León tomorrow with an early start.

There was a robbery at my albergue, and I have heard a lot of reports of injuries and fatalities on the Camino! This reminds us that prayerful starts and days are even more vital.

I tried to pierce the wind and way by moving directly through the space ahead in my step. If only I'd discovered this when I could run. Amazing to think that you can channel your movement forward through what's in front. I never noticed this before, but I guess after walking 400km you'd get it!

My backpack was my home when I travelled around the world in 1990. Now it's my cross that I'm growing to love. Some pay €5 to have their backpack transferred to their next albergue. They complain that they are bound to that destination. Hard as it is to carry, especially when it's stocked with food and water, it must be carried. My feet object the most, by blisters during the day and by aching at night.

Each day has three stages:

1. From early morning until breakfast — most ground is covered as it is cooler and there are lots of pilgrims on the route. It's a race!
2. After the first stop — a little less pilgrims, still a fair distance is travelled, backpack getting heavier. Ok.
3. Into the afternoon — can be hot and a drudge, slower progress, lots of sweat yet you are alone and have the Way. Just you and the Way, with James and John giving great endurance.

I liken these stages and my backpack to Jesus picking up the cross three times. Was each time harder? Certainly, each one is necessary for salvation to be accomplished, and the pilgrim to find a greater love.

Wayside Cross on the Meseta

Day 17

León

22 May (recorded 23 May, 17:32)

It IS just a long walk

Sunrise on the Meseta

Tired, in León, have another big blister having walked 38km, half in the heat. Helped homeless Diego * see afterthoughts. I am staying at the Santa Maria de Carbajal albergue.

* Afterthoughts (on meeting Diego)

I visited the main Correos in León to buy stamps (€1.50 each) for postcards. Although Diego helped translate inside the post office, he approached me outside. He asked if I could give him some money because he is out of work. Spain's large unemployment problem was suddenly in front of me in all its reality.

I invited him to the nearby McDonald's to buy him a meal. I had always intended to give food and drink to those in his situation because money can be misused on drugs or alcohol.

He told me that he had studied the Catholic faith for several years and had learnt English from working in England. He didn't seem sorry for himself nor want to exploit my good nature. Personally, I find it difficult to conceive being in such poverty as to have to beg, with all the shame it can bring to a good soul. Diego wanted to work and said he had a bar prospect to try in Astorga. We exchanged email addresses and on parting I gave him some money. The amount equated to a night or two's accommodation on the Camino, although I knew I would not need to forgo a bed from lack of funds, whereas Diego could now afford a room for a comfy sleep or transport to Astorga.

God puts signs, sometimes in people, in your path and you just need to stop to read them. My meeting with Diego may be one of them because helping the homeless keeps recurring in mine.

In a way, quite incredibly, this has already happened — a charitable arm of Caritas Diocese of Portsmouth reaches homelessness.

Day 18

San Martín del Camino

23 May, 17:32

It IS a walk

A rest day today — only walked 24km. After my rest day experience in Burgos, I decided that I'd continue to walk on rest days, but not for far. This gave me loads of time to sort everything out at the end (approx. 1:30pm finish). I even washed my backpack! The walk was uneventful, and I thank God my new blister was bearable.

I met pilgrims from many nationalities whilst walking and at my albergue — a Colombian based in Spain, Aussies (Moose & Wayne), a Singaporean, Taiwanese, a South Korean and a Swede * see afterthoughts. I posted postcards, a novelty nowadays, to my workplace and the Dominican Sisters at the Priory in the New Forest.

Astorga bound tomorrow — this sounds like a place out of The Chronicles of Narnia. Starting to relax and absorb the Camino again, praise God. Although I am tired!

* Afterthoughts (on fellow pilgrims)

For a few days after León my progress along the Camino slowed down. It was necessary in order to stay at certain destinations without walking too far in any one day. It meant that I criss-crossed over pilgrims along the Camino and started to get to know them. Normally my pace caused me to accelerate away from them — in fact, had I walked on after Sarria I reckon I may have made the podium for the fastest finisher over the age of 50 from the UK for the whole Camino Francés! Thinking back, I did relish the camaraderie this gave. Jesus' disciples had this, and His followers have it today. The common purpose and shared experiences give souls comfort. Humans were built for communion — it's in our Godly DNA.

One criss-cross incident is when I met Wayne in the mountainous cold of O'Cebreiro after the toughest Camino climb, a triple ascent in one. He had joined Moose, his good mate for years, in León. He is a gifted sketch artist. He is not a natural walker, so I remarked on how well he is doing to keep up, only to learn he had got a taxi! Moose by all accounts though was complaining like mad about the climb. This must be a first for an Aussie!

I did appreciate Moose and Wayne. They both had sharp Aussie humour and were a great pair, especially with Moose being so talkative and a relatively new convert to Christianity. His wife is a Pastor. I gave Moose a St. James Cross lapel pin.

Day 19

Astorga

24 May, 16:29

It's NOT just a long walk

In Astorga — what a beautiful place! I'm sitting in Plaza Mayor, enjoying a drink, and waiting for the town hall bells to chime — a mechanism whereby two figures move and strike the bell in turn, like Punch and Judy; they are very quaint and original. It's hot now, 25 degrees Celsius. I walked all 23km this morning without stopping — just one stretch today.

Proudly I was the first to arrive and check in at the albergue San Javier, which is beside the cathedral. This albergue has the most adorable character — a grumpy old hosteller. He wore a suit. After he had given back my pilgrim's credencial and UK passport and I had handed him €8, he bluntly said, "Second floor, shoes there, go on." A great accommodation though, in the roof of an old building yet modernized. I have a single bed in the corner with a shelf.

I did all my washing, called home, and bought betadine (anti-septic) and gauze plasters for my weeping blister.

Antoni Gaudi's Episcopal Palace, next to the cathedral, is impressive. Its gray granite (cream) edifice makes it look like it's straight out of a fairy tale, immaculate. Strikingly, the magnificent buildings that surround its plaza all have different shades of untarnished light-coloured stone. I'm sure when they built Disneyland they would have drawn from references and inspiration here. I hope to visit both the cathedral and the palace, well actually soon.

Plaza Mayor in Astorga.
I loved my time at this place, a gem of the Camino

It's the mountains next — the highest point on the Camino. Strangely I am looking forward to the climbs and the cold! It should be unforgettable. I do need to keep up prayers of guidance and protection throughout as I must keep waiting and be open to God's call.

Day 20

Foncebadón
(5.3km beyond Rabanal)

25 May, 17:33

It is just a long TRUDGE!

John is almost the same length as James now. Everyone loves my "ninja" walking sticks, especially Asian pilgrims. They are "ninja" because whilst praying I tuck them diagonally across my chest pinned to my front by my backpack strap. They become like bamboo swords ready to be drawn — see the photo on the back cover. An Asian pilgrim even stopped me to take a photo of them positioned like this.

I slept badly and left late, at around 7:45am after nearly everyone had already left. Today was hot with a steady climb, followed by a steep 5km climb after Rabanal, quite a trudge.

View of the valley from the annex

I stopped in Foncebadón, which is 1,400+m above sea level, at around 1pm and am staying at a great albergue in an annex with a superb view over the valley.

I am nursing my feet a lot now. Just noticed a crack between my left little toe and the next, which was possibly caused by the Compeed blister plaster, so applied Vaseline to help it heal.

A steep descent tomorrow awaits from 1,500m (highest point on Camino Francés) to 550m. My knees are not looking forward to this test!

I am becoming spiritually dry as the physical side has taken over. The chapel of Ecce Homo, on the outskirts of Astorga, is open very early on for pilgrims as they pass. It provided a refreshing small breeze of life in which to be still with Our Lord. The message on its sign outside, "The faith, foundation of health" could not be more meaningful.

I want every pilgrim to discover faith, to find Jesus and walk with him. To gain immunity to aimless wandering and boredom. With this discovery the need to book ahead a place to stay succumbs to the intuitive spirit of the Camino and trust in God.

"The faith, foundation of health"

Day 21

Columbrianos
(4.7km beyond Ponferrada)

26 May, 19:49

It's NOT just a long walk

Like the Easter candle, both James and John are getting shorter. At the start I could stand and rest on them; now I cannot do this. Also, John, whose metal spike was lost later than James' in sticky mud, is nearly the same length as James. I've bandaged them multiple times to stop the cane splitting. They are still my trusty companions and were sturdy helpers on today's descent from the highest point.

The final ascent, the views, the time at the Cruz de Ferro at 1,504m where everyone leaves a stone from their hometown, and the challenging descent to El Acebo were all uplifting and a better part of the Camino.

Our Lady adorned with flowers

Ponferrada is a lively place on a Sunday. It is a town based around a castle — Castillo de los Templarios is its dominant structure. I only caught the end of Holy Mass in the church near the castle, so I made spiritual union as best I could. I pressed on alone through Ponferrada to end up stopping at a small place (Columbrianos) at 2:40pm. It was just too hot to continue.

I am staying in the San Blas albergue. This albergue has a pilgrim section, a hotel section and a bar for locals. This gives the place a distinctly different ambience than solely pilgrim orientated albergues. After my mandatory shower and clothes wash upon arrival, I sat at the bar to watch Valencia go a goal up against Barcelona in the Spanish Cup Final (the Copa del Rey or King's Cup), then rested earlier than usual.

Cruz de Ferro
I had no stone from home to leave at its base!

These are the last days before Camino Francés finishes and Camino del Norte begins. Lord, thank you for safe passage today.

Day 21 - Columbrianos

Afterthought

From around this point my zeal for the Camino slightly waned; the spark for the divine was dampened within. You may notice this undertone in my words. Nevertheless, I kept on faithfully recording journal entries.

Notes for My Journal:

Not Just a Long Walk

Day 22

Ambasmestas
(13.4km before O'Cebreiro)

27 May, 19:04

It's MUCH MORE than just a long walk

I had a good sleep, so much so that I felt I could walk all day as I set out the next morning! The heat and my feet, which are now improving, sensibly quashed this early eagerness. Walked about 34km until about 4pm and am staying in an idyllic quiet place just off the main highway route, called Ambasmestas.

My albergue, Das Animas, is run by a lovely German couple from Munich. There are only four pilgrims in the dorm, which is quiet, cool and means we have a spacious bottom bunk each.

I have never come across a place quite like Ambasmestas before. It has swallows swooping down its main street and hovering above its streams. They are like a dive-bomber squadron attacking the main street as they swooped down after flies. To enjoy its beauty, I sat and ate my dinner by a stream, and watched the swallows with the odd tiny trout jumping. Blessed indeed. Praise to our God for His Providence.

Most of the day on the Camino was spent with Mick from Cork, Ireland, who also lives in Germany and Spain — he was staying at my albergue and we met just after starting out. We walked together to Villafranca del Bierzo. After this town, the route is on an elevated path with safety barrier for the N-VI road, above and alongside a fast-flowing river. It was easy to keep going with a refreshing breeze.

My morning prayers were missed owing to being with Mick, yet midday prayers, rosary and the Divine Mercy chaplet flowed when he requested that I press on without him. He needed a break from walking as his general health is not the best.

I am thankful for his companionship, caring hostellers and the ups and downs of the Camino!

Idyllic Ambasmestas - streams, tiny trout and squadrons of swallows

Day 23

Triacastela

28 May, 18:31

It is just a long CHALLENGE

The hardest day on three fronts:

1. Woke up with diarrhoea. I had a tiny breakfast, essential toilet stops and ran on empty all day, yet unwisely ate just before finishing.

Afterthought (on a sensible diet)

My diarrhoea was contracted from eating a handful of unpackaged peanuts and raisins. I now realise that one of the raisins was a fly! I bought them because as I entered a shop in El Acebo, the town after the descent two days ago, the owner offered me a peanut from the help-yourself foods. It tasted great so I was lured into buying some.

You always run a risk of contracting an illness while you travel. However, buying and sampling street foods that are unclean and unpackaged should be avoided, or taken with caution at one's own risk.

---

2. A 600m triple ascent is the most challenging on the Camino. Not all could make it; I'm pleased it's over. For those that fish at Hope's Nose, Torquay (a moderately steep cliff with a small rocky path of about 100m in length) this is the same as scaling that climb 50 times over! That's no exaggeration.

3. Once up at 1,200m, it is cold, especially with the piercing breezy wind. This is not enjoyable, so I wanted to get to the other side of the mountain and get down to a warmer level. It's still cold at night though.

All this meant that I pushed past my planned stop at Fonfría in the mountains and kept strong for a further 8.5km despite being drained of energy, to end up walking about 40km.

I had to get to a pharmacy in the next main town, Triacastela (three castles, all now destroyed, yet a pilgrim refuge from the mountains). Now I have two cache solutions (€21.70) to take to clear my diarrhoea and for good intestines! The pharmacist advised to only eat bananas, apples, rice and plain pasta, and drink tea. I checked in at the municipal (Xunta) albergue in Triacastela.

Whilst in the mountains we left Castilla to enter Galicia and passed Alto do San Roque at altitude 1,270m.

Saint Roch healed townships during a Spanish plague in the 14th century and was miraculously healed when he contracted the deadly disease by his dog licking his sores. Consequently, at the time lots of towns replaced their patron, Santiago, in favour of San Roque.

The spiritual way was lost a lot today owing to these challenges. I still offered up much in my devotions as I walked. Hoping I will have the strength to get to Sarria tomorrow and recover for the Camino del Norte.

God gives many crosses. His blessings and grace give much, much more to be grateful for.

Afterthoughts (on God's message from this Camino)

As my Camino progressed the spiritual path became more and more obscure. Early on I noticed the great number of pilgrims and kept questioning my Lord God as to why. I had come for close union with Him, and not His people. The message, however, was persistent — if you want to know and be in relationship with me, you must also be with my people. Each day they were there — pilgrims journeying side by side — how could I miss God's message? It was undeniable! My conscious and subconscious awakened fully my heart to people. It was impossible not to see this message with so many pilgrims. Their varying states of life and formative maturity. It is my clear takeaway for life from God on this Camino. Thank you, Lord.

To reflect a little more, we have the two simplest and greatest commandments from Jesus, to love God and to love our neighbour as Jesus loves us. I recall once being reminded by a parishioner that she was there physically, "pinch me" she said, "I am beside you." We can't see God, but we can see and interact with each other. This is similar to the wake up to the person in my neighbour, as in the parable of the Good Samaritan, that shall forever be etched in my memory from this Camino. It's good to travel the Way.

Notes for My Journal:

Day 24

Sarria
buses to Ribadeo

29 May, 11:26

It IS just a long walk

God gives real-life angels. In my tiny dorm of four, there was one — a sweet lady, Irena, from near Johannesburg, South Africa. I mentioned my diarrhoea and she said she is a pharmacist and gave me her anti-diarrhoea tablets. What the pharmacy had given did not combat the diarrhoea. I took two tablets and must take one every time I poo! I couldn't sleep either — my toes were too cold despite wearing three pairs of socks. Eventually, I did fall asleep at 2am. Got up at 5:30am and ate a banana and apple as prescribed.

I left the albergue and walked the 18km to Sarria, arriving at around 10:30am. I was then sick in a café owing to the fresh apple and felt better for it. I found the church in Sarria where I first started in March 2012 and thereby connected the Ways * see the related story.

It's complete, my soul can rest easier with my Lord.

I am currently waiting in Sarria autobus station to get the 12:25 Monbus to Lugo. I could not contemplate continuing along the Camino Francés from Sarria into the busiest stretch.

This next 100km stretch is "overwalked" and strips away the whole essence of the Camino. If walked again the beauty with which I found it, and God found me on my first Camino, would have been killed. As planned, a new Camino, the Norte awaits.

God is good, even though I'm running on empty and want to sleep and rest.

*At the church in Sarria
where my first Camino started*

Recorded later 1 June, 15:36:
Arrived from Lugo in Ribadeo with a good bus connection on Arriva bus at around 3:15pm.

The pensión (guest house) I had booked through www.booking.com whilst on the coach was 8km from the city centre of Ribadeo, not in it as described, so I had to immediately try to cancel the booking. I walked to the centre only to find all the shops were closed for siesta, including the Ribadeo Tourist Office. I needed to wait until 4pm to find accommodation. However, I looked up and saw a pensión sign just off the central plaza. I made an inquiry. After ringing to summon the old lady who runs it, who couldn't understand any English, she said "Peregrino €15." Not bad for the first night in a single room with a double bed and clean sheets.

Day 24 - Sarria

After visiting the tourist office, I went to the hospital to see a doctor. In the diagnosis of acute diarrhoea, I received an injection in my butt, tiorfan tablets and a drink to take (1 litre every 24 hours), both for up to five days. All that the pharmacist gave in Triacastela to cure me was useless and wasted.

The doctor was quite a character — she "kinda told yer" to get well! I was instructed to fast until noon the following day, put on a strict diet and told to rest for 2-3 days. It's been difficult getting the foods for the diet and cooking with no facilities at my pensión.

Notes for My Journal:

* Related story (on sourcing a credencial on my first Camino)

A credencial is a kind of pilgrim's passport that is stamped on check in at albergues, hostels or hotels. Stamps may also be collected at cafes, restaurants, chapels, churches, or cathedrals along the Way. The Pilgrims' Reception Office in Santiago will take these stamps as evidence of having completed the Way and duly award a devotional certificate of accomplishment, called a 'Compostela.' For a small fee, the office can also issue a certificate that records the distance walked or cycled, the starting town, date and the Camino route that was taken * see afternote.

Upon arrival by bus in Sarria on my first Camino in March 2012, after climbing the steps up to Iglesia de Santa Mariña to buy a credencial, I found the church was closed. My new guidebook said I could also get a credencial at Monasterio de Santa Maria Madalena, so I walked along the Way to the end of the town trying to follow the map. Eventually, I found the monastery, but I could not see anybody, nor did I know how to contact the people inside. The place seemed as if it was closed.

I decided to start out and walked down the small hill out of the town. I was desperately keen to experience walking the Camino, but at the bottom of this hill, I stopped beside a derelict albergue. I knew I could not go on without a credencial before I left Sarria, so reluctantly I walked back up the hill and asked the children in the nearby school if they could help me. A couple of teenagers understood what I wanted and asked that I wait until they finished school.

Day 24 - Sarria 81

They then walked with me to the monastery. As they stepped inside the entrance, they immediately pulled a rope to summon the attendant. "Great," I thought, "now I can start."

We waited but nobody came. Quite some time passed. The teenagers gave up waiting and explained I must continue waiting, somebody will come. They did not know how long I must wait. "Never mind," I thought, "now I may not start" (as the walk to Portomarin was over 23km and I could not set out too late). I resigned myself to this when all-of-a-sudden the door opened. The attendant entered and sold me my credencial for €1. I can go now.

It was at this point that he asked if I would like to visit the chapel inside the monastery. My heart overflowed with joy at this offer. I stepped through the door into the monastery and walked with him to the chapel. As we got there, he left me.

I walked to the front of the altar, knelt before the tabernacle and wept, and wept and wept. To think that I'd almost given up, in what was at the time, the alien territory of the Camino. Why did I doubt Our Lord? Then He, through the attendant, had suddenly opened what seemed like every door and had given an opportunity to be before Him. "Ask and you will receive; seek and you will find; knock and the door will be opened" (Matthew 7:7). Everything was in place after leaving this chapel as my spirit and soul were also ready to begin. I had been enormously blessed in this moment. I thanked the attendant and set off.

A few days later, over lunch, I was chatting to another pilgrim who was a wonderful light. I mentioned that I had wept at the chapel inside the Monastery of St. Mary Magdalene. On hearing this he gave me the St. James Cross lapel pin.

* Afternote (on certificate rules): The Pilgrims' Office will register the distance travelled on a "chronological and geographical" journey to Santiago de Compostela. "It is understood that the pilgrimage starts at one point and from there you come to visit the Tomb of St. James" (ref. www.oficinadelperegrino.com/en). So, if, for whatever reason, you switch Camino routes along the Way, your starting place, routes, and the combined distance walked or cycled will not be acknowledged.

Despite my pleading that I had unequivocally started at St. Jean Pied de Port, rules are rules; only my time on the Camino del Norte, that had lengthened my Camino by 80km, could be recorded on my accreditation certificates. The administrators would not concede a pilgrim starts where, in the spirit of faith, his journey is first undertaken.

Recovery Days 25, 26 & 27

Ribadeo
(on the Camino del Norte)

30 - 31 May & 1 June (recorded 1 June, 15:36)

It is just a long WAY

Just washed everything — sleeping sheet, hat, fleece, windproof, pyjamas, clothes — ready for Camino del Norte. It's good to get everything clean because with all the fitness training I've done over the years my body is efficient and sweats a lot in the heat and whilst climbing hills. Unfortunately, I had the runs again this morning, but I must walk tomorrow — not good news!

The town of Ribadeo is by the sea, well it's just inland on a big estuary, but from the beautiful marina, you can see the open sea. You hear the gulls. It is quiet and you get no sense that it's a Camino town.

Surprisingly, near the marina, I spotted rods in a first-class fishing tackle-store (www.capturaspesca.com) and took time to select a rod and reel for mackerel fishing at Hope's Nose, Torquay. To avoid carrying these large and long items they were sent on to Santiago de Compostela, to the barber friend of Lucia, the store owner, for me to collect from him on arrival.

It's the European Champions League final tonight, Liverpool

v Tottenham, who whilst I was on the Camino both remarkably overcame first-leg defeats against the odds to make the final. It's the first time that there have been all English European Champions League and UEFA Europa League finalists (Chelsea v Arsenal). I hope to find a place to watch the game later. It's been a year since I was with my son Andrew on the Portuguese Way in Padrón watching the same final, Liverpool v Real Madrid.

Marina in Ribadeo

The spiritual path seems to have gone out of focus. These last few days that beckon, this new way on the Norte, with far fewer pilgrims and spectacular countryside, with a fitter body, I pray will lead me closer to God.

Day 28

Lourenzá

2 June, 19:39

It's not just a long walk; it is a PILGRIMAGE

What a contrast. Camino Francés, hundreds of pilgrims; Camino del Norte, just a few. Camino Francés, mainly noisy and hot; Camino del Norte, peace, nature, open fields, and views. What a contrast. For the last 40km, the Camino del Norte joins the Camino Francés — will we notice this change!?!

Today's stage from Ribadeo (the last and only sight of the sea) to Lourenzá is hilly, as is most of Galicia. It is good to walk again, even though I'm not fully over my diarrhoea. I stupidly had cream soup, which has milk, and I guess that's what's kept it! Now I have the tastiest meals: plain rice Spanish style and pre-toasted white bread. I am eating like a king; not! The horrible prescribed drink is over — I don't have to take it again thankfully. Yet it may have given me some energy. We'll find out tomorrow. Fortunately, it's only a 24km stage. The days after could be a lot longer and I could need food for energy.

Lourenzá is a quiet place and has a magnificent site, which is shown on the cover of the guide to the Northern Way. It is the 10th century Benedictine Monasterio de San Salvador, a national historical monument. Apart from the impressive façade, there didn't seem much else as I walked around its walls, although I was not able to enter.

I was the first pilgrim to arrive at my albergue, and although it cost €13, it is the cleanest and best that I've stayed at. Thank you, Lord, it's a perfect place.

It's Sunday so everywhere is closed, and I just missed Holy Mass again at 1pm. Mass times are haphazard from town to town. Why couldn't it have been at 2pm?

Most walkers on the Norte are German — about two-thirds. Despite this, I'm yet to meet one from Stuttgart, where Libby, my daughter, is working. Libby has a love of the Camino, having walked it solo when she was younger. I also met a Portuguese couple today who walk a Camino route every year, yet not for religious purposes, even though they believe.

There is more time to reflect whilst on the Way of the Norte. Thanks be to God.

Notes for My Journal:

Day 29

Abadín

3 June, 15:44

It's NOT just a long walk

Lourenzá to Mondoñedo, then to Abadín, two stages in the Galician drizzle.

Today I walked in drizzle all day. Refreshing, yet you cannot see much in the shroud of the mountain mist. After a café stop by the plaza opposite the cathedral in Mondoñedo, I followed the Camino signs and unintentionally ended up on the alternative ("complementary") way to Abadín. It's apparently an easier route yet longer.

It was another day of testing terrain. The first two days on the Norte in Galicia are the most difficult. Although tomorrow is 40km on easier terrain!

I managed to wash and dry all my clothes despite the lack of sun. We are all hoping this weather is not the norm for the next few days! Dry would be good.

Recorded at 17:26

The rain in Spain falls mainly on Galicia! This hilly and undulating region is not "on the plain" yet gets more than its fair share of rain. In contrast, the rest of Spain was hot and sunny, approaching record high temperatures causing forest fires. As a result, my recommendation is to avoid walking the Camino in Galicia over the first weeks of June. It's not only I that have found this; it's a notoriously wet time of year!

The mountains in mist

Notes for My Journal:

Day 30

Miraz

4 June, 21:51

It's NOT just a long walk

A choice — to walk 20km (Vilalba) or 40km (Baamonde)? I chose the latter because the terrain is flat. After a sleepless night, I woke early, cooked minestrone soup and left Abadín at 6:30am, knowing the distance ahead.

It's the Norte with very few pilgrims, so the whole day is made so much easier and enjoyable by ambling along conversing with three engaging pilgrims:

- Christina from Germany (before and to Vilalba) who was bubbly and had cherished walking the Norte along the coast.

- Marianne from Mexico (before and to Baamonde) for whom this was her first Camino experience, opportunely taken on the back of a working trip to London. She and her brother walked too far on the first day and he suffered an injury that stopped him walking any further. We shared life experiences. This was an unexpected tonic to us both — it's great to talk openly! Her profession is filmmaking.

- Lorenzo from Italy (after Baamonde until his pre-booked albergue). With him being in his late twenties we were able to speedily cover ground in the rain. Fortunately, I met him a day later in my dorm at Sobrado dos Monxes as I had resolved to

Not Just a Long Walk 90

give him a St James Cross lapel pin if our paths crossed, such was our instant bond. At a café stop in Vilalba I gave a lapel pin to Christina too.

When I got to Baamonde I discovered that the big municipal albergue had a kitchen but nothing to cook with, and the Hostel was €25 with no kitchen. So I decided to push on from 3:50 to 7pm to Miraz, another 15km, to stay at the albergue run by the Confraternity of St James, for which I have kept my membership ever since my first Camino * see afterthoughts. A staggering total of 55km was walked from 6:30am to 7pm, my record!

All weathers were encountered today — overcast, drizzle, sun, cloud, and rain. Thankfully, all-of-a-sudden in Vilalba, when the sun came out, the Camino was back! I had been starting to see it as a long walk! Maybe it coincided with my return from illness. Yet the zest to walk the Camino was restored in an instant. Why was it ever lost? I must have lost sight of the beauty of God's love and not remained still enough to allow Him to seep into my heart.

The longest ever day so far. God is good.

* Afterthoughts (on 'donativo' albergues)

'Donativo' albergues are ones that only accept donations for a night's accommodation. They often also offer communal meals.

They are operated by organisations that seek to keep a refuge open to pilgrims on the Way. These organisations typically include parishes and national confraternities, such as The Confraternity of St. James in the UK, and a few remaining towns (municipals). Their upkeep is subsidised by the members of the organisation and their helpers are normally volunteers. These volunteers show a wonderful welcome and loving care to pilgrims.

However, owing to growing private competition they are becoming fewer and fewer. Many pilgrims call ahead as they want to guarantee their bed for a night and will not leave staying at 'donativos' to chance. This fear, therefore, means that they almost always have beds available and are sometimes completely empty, even at busier times on the Camino.

The 'donativos' of the Camino are the Gospel equivalents to the stable in Bethlehem. As Joseph and Mary found, they provide a roof overhead to a 'family' of pilgrims who are looking for a place to stay. These pilgrims are joined by the company of shepherds in the form of their hostellers and like-natured pilgrims drawn to the same place. They are treasured places.

It's important to be aware of the predicament of 'donativo' albergues in the high-tech world of smartphones. A world in which they now coexist. We can be supportive, appreciative and amenable to the service and genuine hospitality they offer to pilgrims.

Can you make this *donativo* too?

If it were possible it would be my wish that this book is also 'donativo.' With this in mind, please enter the spirit of the Camino through the scene created in the next paragraphs.

Imagine that you are tired from your day's walking. That you are under the sheltering wing of a hosteller and are resting on your comfortable bed. That you have facilities to cook, eat and wash and fellow pilgrims for company.

Now pause to thank God for this place he has given; for the day's blessings and encounters. As you lie there, dwell on the sacrifices that your host has made to keep the space open to you and other pilgrims. Remain still for a moment longer to reflect further on our love of neighbour.

As you emerge from this scene, please leave a small 'donativo' as moved by your heart with a charity below by visiting their website to donate.

ANCOP: www.cfcancop.org

Caritas: www.portsmouthdiocese.org.uk/caritas

Missionaries of the Poor:
www.missionariesofthepoor.org

These are the three works of faith this journal helps support. Please include their mission in your prayers.

Day 31

Sobrado dos Monxes

5 June, 14:15

It's NOT just a long walk

James and John are getting shorter, yet they are still "good and faithful servants" (Matthew 25:21). Like the Easter candle, they will live forever in my memory.

Today the weather gave everything again, sun and rain — it's Galicia!

I'm currently waiting in a bar in Sobrado dos Monxes for the albergue in the monastery to open at 4pm. The first time I've had to wait two hours for one to open! Hopefully, I can wash my clothes, dry them, and cook there, as I've just bought some food from the supermarket.

The Camino was exceptionally beautiful today: crossing rocky faces, down small tree-shadowed descents, a lake with the sounds of "croaky" frogs, very peaceful to start with. Another part of the Camino to thank God for.

The notice on the door to the monastery and albergue - its opening times

I met Ericka from Germany, who seems to have come to terms with her divorce after many years of marriage, and the young Sophia and Diana from Barcelona.

Bra straps! Having walked nearly all the Camino with my backpack on the back and a day bag on the front (to access sunglasses, hat, sunscreen, money, water, guide, etc. when needed), I've lost count of the times I've adjusted my day bag strings/straps to be around my shoulders, rather than down my arms. Adjusting them feels good and helps with comfort. However, just pause to think of the women that must constantly adjust, deal with, and put up with bra straps. It's given me greater regard for their plight!

You never know what life has in store yet it's a whole load more perfect with You, Lord.

Recorded later 6 June, 19:47:

Staying at the monastery in Sobrado is special. It's now a world heritage site. The altar and place of worship inside the monastery is vast and totally bare. They are repairing its towers outside. Apparently, this is painstakingly slow work.

I bought two rosaries with alternating cream, tan, brown and black beads from the plush gift shop inside the grounds. These rosaries stood out from every item on display.

Remarkably, I officially flew the flag for the UK — I was the only British pilgrim walking the Norte according to another pilgrim who had walked from Irun at its start. I verified her observation because I too had not met any Brits on the Norte either.

In the communal area, there is a surprisingly modern piece of art in the most unlikely place — an image of the Cross set in the kitchen alcove. It greatly impressed and could easily have gone unnoticed. I resolved to share it with the leaders of CFC Youth for Christ on my return, so excitedly mentioned this to Lorenzo, who in turn explained the message behind The Calling of St. Matthew masterpiece by Caravaggio.

Day 31 - Sobrado dos Monxes

The Camino Way of the Cross

Afterthoughts (on this image)

It has barbed wire for the arms of the Cross, with some wool impaled on the barbs; a yellow Camino waymarker on the base of the wooden upright pointing to the place where Jesus had to go; the acronym "INRI" (Jesus the Nazarene, King of the Jews) written in the purple framework, the Lenten colour of spiritual preparation for the coming joy of Easter.

If ever you could portray the Way of the Camino in the Way of a modern Cross that depicts the path walked by the Holy One of Israel, it is in this artwork.

In particular, the barbed wire, which is used to keep people out, is the place for the outstretched arms of Jesus, opened in suffering to bridge and endure the pain of original sin, so the original innocence of humanity may once again be claimed by those who believe in Him, the Word made flesh (John 1:14) — those who follow God's Word made man, whose Spirit is alive and present in the Church today.

The barren altar inside the monastery at Sobrado dos Monxes

Day 32

Monte do Gozo
(4.9km before Santiago
de Compostela)

6 June, 19:47

It IS just a long walk

Almost there! Today was a marathon — arguably three legs in one, I walked almost 60km! I know that I did want to skip this last leg of the Camino Francés or blast through it. However, the fact that I did cover the distance in one day was not intentional.

I left Sobrado dos Monxes at 7:15am for the last 20km on the Norte. The Norte joined the Francés at Arzúa. After Arzúa my plan was to walk on about 10km on the Francés and stop. However, both albergues that I tried to stay at were full ("completo") and no others clearly presented themselves as I walked on.

The number of pilgrims — so, so, so many, loads in the rain too. One lady had booked her accommodation a year before! What chance do we have to find a place to sleep on this stretch? I told this lady that pre-booking "kills the Camino", to trust in God is a basic lesson of the Camino. She did not react.

I doubt she understood.

The town O Pedrouzo is off route and I figured most must be pre-booked there. As I continued, a pilgrim even waved and shouted at me, "O Pedrouzo, O Pedrouzo" as if everyone is expected to stop there before Santiago.

I walked on a long way, in the torrential rain to start with, to the municipal albergue at Monte do Gozo with 400 beds. I was guaranteed a bed there, plus it's a great albergue. This place, Monte do Gozo ("Hill of Joy"), is so named because it's where pilgrims, after walking for many weeks or months, gave cries of joy on their first sight of the spires of the cathedral of Santiago.

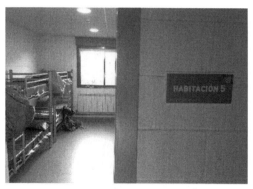

Sanctuary at Monte do Gozo

The rain in Spain most definitely falls mainly in Galicia in June, and it was windy. Now I have some blisters from my drenched, squelchy shoes. The longest day!

If you have not already gathered, this was an extremely testing day. It was unforgettable and the greatest character-building day of my whole Camino * see the related story. God tested and helped find new bounds to my inner greatness (the spirit of God within). It's a day that had been pre-planned from the beginning.

However, this last leg of the Camino Francés did not exceed

Day 32 - Monte do Gozo 99

my low expectations regarding how commercial it has become. I am sure it is an experience for most (those who claim, "I did the Camino") rather than one that is life-changing and one in which God's purpose is sought.

I am feeling a lot better now at the end of the day as I've eaten twice — microwave potatoes and meat with cheese roll from a fellow peregrino. Then a burger in the local bar that I ate at in March 2012. Santiago tomorrow; recovery tonight!!!

Notes for My Journal:

* Related story (on character found in *the face-off*)

On this longest day, there was one scene worthy of mention. This is my Agincourt moment. It happened at about 5:30pm in the afternoon.

To set the scene...

The whole stretch after O Pedrouzo was eerily surreal. There should have been hundreds of walkers on these final few kilometres that descend on Santiago. Yet there were none. None at all, hardly a living soul. It was like a ghost town! There was even less activity than when I walked through the area in March 2012 (this was at a time when there were a lot fewer walkers and the Way was just awakening to a new season). However, I did enjoy the tranquillity that God had now given me through my determination to keep going. I was always aware of the sanctuary to be found on the horizon at Monte do Gozo by pressing on.

I had walked all day, hardly stopping, through about four hours of torrential rain. The heaviest rain I can ever remember, with nothing except my poncho to cover me. I had no coat nor umbrella. Fortunately, my backpack was watertight owing to the rain cover stored in a compartment at its base. All the time I was concerned my mobile phone would get wet and cease working. Its electronics were failing causing it to flicker and go blank. I thought I might lose access to the photos that I had taken along the Way, as well as the ability to contact anyone. My trousers, shoes, socks and feet were drenched.

So, I came to a long straight road with huge deep puddles, likes ponds, on either side of the road and a narrow dry patch in the centre of the road to walk through. There was no means of walking around on the flooded non-existent path on either side either. The only route forward was the narrow dry patch in the centre of the road. A car appeared in the distance. I instantly calculated that as we moved toward each other, that we would meet at this only right of passage in the centre of the road.

In my dejected yet obstinate state, I was not going to back down. That is my right of passage. "I have had enough today," I thought, "You are not going through that space before me." It's my Agincourt moment.

This is when the English bowmen, exhausted and downtrodden from fleeing the French forces, drew a line in the mud of Agincourt and stood their ground. "Come at us, armoured cavalry, we will not move." No longer fearful, they stood fast, knowing they could launch arrows in seconds as the horsemen got stuck in the muddy field. They were victorious in the courage they found in the character of a downtrodden spirit.

Never before had I confronted a car with such determination to not give ground as at that moment. Needless to say, in my face-off, I won. The car sped to a halt and waited for me to pass.

There is a conversion note too to be found in this confrontation. In this desperation the finding of our character is revealed. We can find God within us. When we have nothing left to keep going on our own steam we are broken down to submission. We are opened to God with his strength and power in this surrender. This is affirmed by the Lord to St. Paul, "My grace is sufficient for you, for power is made perfect in weakness." (2 Corinthians 12:9)

In this moment I was broken by this miserable time on the Way. Yet I found a resolve and optimism to break out of my protective self by confronting the car. I was no longer afraid of the consequence of moving toward it. Death at worst if the car had continued to speed toward me * see afternote. I surrendered to the outcome. My brokenness had brought a new and renewed trust, need and belief in the Almighty.

It's like this with every resistant soul. They just have to allow themselves to surrender everything to God. Instead, they go on stubbornly fighting the One whose capacity to love and care for them is boundless and infinite. They find ways to convince themselves they are clever and in control of their lives. When in fact, they are dependent on God's Providence. He is Wisdom and has control.

Please reflect on these thoughts about my memorable Agincourt moment.

* Afternote: Consider in the light of this, that a Dutch pilgrim opted to walk off the Camino path, on the road to avoid uneven ground underfoot, and was hit by a car and killed. This was reported by her national press. Lord, may her soul rest in peace. Amen.

Day 33

Santiago de Compostela

7 June, 08:56

It is a PILGRIMAGE with a DESTINATION

It's accomplished!

The small walk into Santiago was relaxing. I'm now sitting in the main plaza outside Santiago Cathedral watching the tour groups, pilgrims and locals. Most are getting their arrival photo. The repair work outside on the Door of Glory is finished, and now work on the inside of the cathedral has caused the Pilgrim Mass to move elsewhere, all aimed for completion by the next Saint's year in 2021.

Group celebrations on arrival

It's 10am. What's next?

This is the last entry and the end of this Camino journey.

Epilogue

It took two months to dawn on me after returning that the duration of my Camino was 33 days. The length of this journal is 33 days. This is the length of Jesus' time on earth — 33 short years. It is the proper duration to walk the full Camino Francés. Despite my great zeal and tempo how did God know to temper and perfectly orchestrate my journey? I am awestruck when I sit back to take this in — His hand is in everything!

Before going back to conclude Fr. Mark's observation from my preparation days, if you recall my opening thoughts were on the importance of recognising and responding to our own vision. This led me to realise how much our vision can shape, change and lift us when we make its pursuit our priority. In particular if it's drawing us to the Camino. This, in turn, will make us witnesses to where our vision has taken us. By the way, Jesus adores witnesses — He loves those who are able to see and testify to His presence and action in their life.

For even more food for thought we will explore this theme a little further by considering this, "they lifted up their eyes, and saw no one but Jesus." (Matthew 17:8). You may think that is a strange reference from holy scripture to use. It gets to the main point though. After Christ's self-revelation of His glory at the Transfiguration where, "his face shone like the sun and his garments became white as light" His closest disciples, including James, had been given this glorious vision of the future. They also saw the reality after, "no one but Jesus" in front of them.

There's no doubt that we are blessed to have our vision of God — it draws us towards Him. With this vision directed toward God, we can see God's plan in our lives. It's a vision that can be crystallised in the path of relational self-discovery in the Way of the Camino. We may not only discover who we truly are, but we may also discover our vision and be given the fortitude to remain with Our Lord on its path. Moreover, for some of us, the haze around our vision may also be cleared — Christ's glorious guiding light shines brighter into our purpose than before we journeyed. All of this coming from our own vision.

So, let's now move on to my brief meeting with Fr. Mark along the mini Camino (from Reading to Southampton) where he commented that the Camino would bring lots of experiences of meeting people along the Way. If you recall I questioned his remark. There must be more. Now, having journeyed, I can say that Fr. Mark is right. It almost totally sums up the Camino.

The Camino is in a nutshell just that — a series of experiences, of many encounters that somehow live with us. The places and the challenges are ingredients, yet it's God that made us in His image. The Camino is made by the people, the pilgrims. It makes you appreciate every individual that God puts on your path. Whether they reciprocate or not. Whether they are open to our embrace or beyond its outreach. It is with the unconditional love of our neighbour after all that we become Jesus' disciples. The heart of Jesus' great Apostle is warmed when this happens.

Jesus' salvific sacrificial love is also seen along the whole Way. Every wayside crucifix, with stones laid in prayer at its base by a pilgrim, is a reminder. From these constant

Epilogue 107

encounters, through people and signs, acceptance of God's love and mercy can take permanent root. The Camino then becomes more than just a long walk because it has transformed our hearts too.

Fr. Mark asked me to pray for him. I did.

I could easily have left this Epilogue at the previous sentence. However, I need to share these next insights and reflections even if you have already read or heard them in other forms. Most of the time it's good to be reminded!

They say that along the Way the journey alternates from yourself (the inside) to your surroundings (the outside), back and forth whilst walking. However, there is also another dimension — that of God's constant gaze (from our outside to our inside). With this dimension, the Camino becomes not so much seeking inside or outside, but instead a place in which we allow ourselves to be found. The expression "let go and let God" does not quite convey this observation. It's more "go and let God." This is because it's on the Camino that the true pilgrim has made himself available to be observed and deeply accessed by a loving and merciful God.

Finally, they also say that God does not give what you want, but what you need. This is certainly true of every Camino journey if we are rightly disposed before embarking on the Way. As I found, we cannot expect too much of our venture for we do not know how, when or where God will act, yet it's certainly true that if we look with eyes of faith, we will see His message on the Camino. He will have given us what we need to go forward in our lives. Therefore, we must not forget the Camino of life.

Do think "outside the box" (of the Camino de Santiago) about every avenue of your being as you pause to ponder this parting thought:

What door do I need to open in my life for my own great Camino adventure?

Whatever your answer, go!!! Time stands still on the Camino, and in time we are born, it's where we find life.

A note to some who would like to walk the Camino yet are immediately defeated at the prospect of walking. Nearly every testimony made is always that each day is among the best and most memorable of times. On my Camino I walked with a 72-year-old Spanish pilgrim who had hip replacements — for him 20km was far. I also met young pilgrims who restrict their distance to 10km a day. If you operate within your own capacity and prepare, what is to stop you, other than you?

Let's finish with a prayer. This is my prayer thinking of everything that's happened and everything that is still to come...

Closing Prayer

Lord, thank you for the shared experiences and reflections in this journal.

Help us to listen to your call in our own vision and walk the path that you want us to walk, as we journey in your Creation through varying states and stages of life and understanding toward your Kingdom. Guide us in your light to follow your will and purpose for our lives.

By your daily presence, calm our spirit, give us your peace and fill us with renewed joy, hope, and grace to always live in a way that is pleasing to You.

As our brother and greatest friend, stir our spirit to venture beyond a comfortable existence and find our inner greatness that gives glory to You, especially if it's the Camino that summons this discovery. Stir our hearts too, so that in our every move we never cease to desire to know, love and serve You, your Church and your people.

We place all our trust in You.

This prayer we make in the mighty name of Our Lord Jesus

Epilogue 109

Christ, who lives and reigns with you and the Holy Spirit, one God, forever and ever. Amen
Our Father...

As we part, I wish you a good life. Buen Camino.

Not Just a Long Walk

Acknowledgements

Firstly, lastly and always, I am grateful to the Holy Spirit for the gifts that moved me to stand firm and sacrifice what is necessary to open a period to walk the full Camino, and for God's protection throughout of my family and friends.

I am thankful too to...

Vivian, my wife, for letting me get on with and not questioning, even understanding, why I would be restless if I did not go on this great Camino adventure. Also, for supporting every step.

Lilia Maragun, my sister in Christ, who I could not help while away when the Home Office suddenly compelled her to return to the Philippines despite her love for this country and its people. This came after living in the UK for 8 years. I am sorry.

Rev. Fr. Stan Gibzinski, the priest at Our Lady of Peace & Bl. Dominic Barberi parish, Reading, who knows me so well that he recognises the seeking of my real identity.

Smith Eufracio and Allyza Escabarte, CFC Youth for Christ leaders, for their prayers and acceptance of my absence from their side in ministry.

Linda Heath, my Line Manager at work, for allowing my extended break.

My daughter, Libby, and my good friends, John Parten and

John Allinson of Our Lady of Peace & Bl. Dominic Barberi parish, Reading and Paul Jinks, husband of Cora, my sister in Christ, for reading and giving excellent critical comment and observations.

Adrian Croft, a treasured friend, for his editorial strokes, especially in the use of Spanish accents.

John Parten, for guiding me through the self-publication process, including how to code html (Hypertext Markup Language).

Brian Aquino and Richna Uy of CFC YCOM (Youth Communications) ministry for their awesome design of the journal's cover, and Richna for encouraging the addition of prayers that led to the 'Prayerful Findings' appendix.

Angela Wills of English Martyrs parish, Reading, who walked the Camino for a cause and in so doing drew to my awareness that such a pilgrim path existed. Without her announcement it may have been years before I discovered the Way, although I forget the action of God who steers all our paths and knew that I would follow this direction!

And lastly, I am indebted to my trusty companions, the ever-dependable James and John, who made it to the journey's end.

My family (Libby, Andrew and Vivian) in Muxia on the Camino Finisterre

Appendix 1 - Origins of the Camino

On the pages that follow are extracts from the leaflet on the modern paintings by artists: Paulo Guilherme Vieira Marques and Julio Cesar Quaresma Caravelli from St. Benedict Studio, Brazil. These paintings adorn the Shrine of St. James at St. James Church, Reading, England. They give insight into the origins of the Camino.

Before reading the text from the leaflet that describes the painted scenes, please pause to examine these images in order to absorb the story of the events brilliantly portrayed by this art. Each painting is shown outright before the text is given.

The Legend of St. James wall painting

Origins of the Camino

It is said that St. James (Sant-Iago), the apostle, the brother of John, came to Spain to preach Christianity. He returned to Jerusalem and was one of the first Apostles to be beheaded by Herod for his faith.

After his death his followers put his body into a rudderless boat, and this was carried by angels and the wind to the coast of north-western Spain. The bodies of St. James and two of his followers were buried at Iria Flavia (Padrón) in Galicia, Northern Spain. The burial site was forgotten for some 800 years. The tomb was rediscovered and the relics authenticated by the local bishop. At the time the church fostered devotion to relics of holy people as a way to be close to God and so began the pilgrimage to Santiago de Compostela. In time it became a rival to those to Rome and Jerusalem. For many centuries interest waned but in recent years a very high number of people are now walking the Way of St. James, the Camino de Santiago de Compostela to visit the great Cathedral and pray at the Tomb of St. James.

Tradition has it that St. James miraculously appeared as a knight on horseback to fight for the Spanish army during the legendary battle of Clavijo against the Moors, originally from Africa. Today a visitor to Spain will see the contribution of Islam as well as that of the Jewish community in the amazing architecture and culture in so many of the cities.

The feast day of St. James is celebrated on 25th July.

The Camino de Santiago wall painting

Origins of the Camino

Ever since the Middle Ages the scallop shell has been the symbol of those on pilgrimage to the shrine of St. James in Santiago. It is worn by pilgrims and can be used when thirsty to drink water. The scallop shell is marked with the sword-shaped cross of St. James.

In the middle of the panel is an outline of the great Cathedral in Santiago, where the body of St. James lies. Above the building are stars, reminders that a bright star showed the place where St. James' body was found and that pilgrims were said to be as numerous as the stars of the Milky Way.

The Way of St. James or Camino de Santiago is one of the great Christian pilgrimages of the world. These days thousands of people walk the route. For those on the walk it is not only an experience of great endurance, the opportunity to enjoy the scenery of the area but also a journey inward. People of all cultures and faiths are attracted to the challenge of walking this historic route.

Helpful advice about the pilgrimage is available from the Confraternity of Saint James which has a strong link with this parish (St. James RC Church, Reading). The Great Abbey of Reading was a place of medieval pilgrimage as it held the relic of the hand of St. James which is now kept in St. Peter's Church, Marlow.

For more information about the Confraternity and the pilgrimage to Santiago de Compostela visit www.csj.org.uk or tel: +44 (0)20 7928 9988.

Appendix 2 - Faith in Action

Love for the poor is inspired by the example of Jesus in his constant concern for the poor. Jesus said, "Whatever you have done to the least of my brethren, you have done to me" (Matthew 25:40). Hence, the innate desire to carry out and support corporal and spiritual works of mercy through the offering of this journal.

Aptly, it is written of those who respond to Jesus with love, "the warmhearted man will be blessed since he shares his bread with the poor." (Proverbs 22:9)

On the pages that follow are details of the three charities, their projects, the people (Our Lord's people) that all the proceeds of this journal will benefit.

ANCOP
Cornerstone

This extract from my GoFundMe page — Camino Steps for Cornerstone — explains:

I invite you to encourage my Camino journey by giving to less privileged children in accord with God's plan to share resources and blessings. For love is not love if it's not shared.

To fulfil this ANCOP (ANswering the Cry of the Poor) is a charity that through "Cornerstone", its Couples for Christ partnership programme in the Philippines, aims to reach out to elementary children in public schools who are slow readers by giving reading tutorials and value formation. The very name Cornerstone inspires this promise to assist these children because it refers to Christ Himself (Mark 12:10-11).

Go to **www.cfcancop.org** to donate or for further information.

Missionaries of the Poor Mercy Village

Situated in a 4-hectare wooded property in the municipality of Compostela, 25km north of Cebu City in the Philippines. Mercy Village is where 35 poor boys and special-needs children call their home.

Administered by the religious of the Missionaries of the Poor, this "village" strives to offer a holistic care for these needy children, some of whom are orphans and/or abandoned, with academic education, skills training and value formation. The aim is not only to enable them for a better tomorrow for themselves, but also to be compassionate and responsible "neighbours" to their fellow human beings and the environment.

Go to **www.missionariesofthepoor.org** to donate or for further information.

Caritas Diocese of Portsmouth

The meaning of the word "Caritas" is the practical expression of Christian love.

Caritas Diocese of Portsmouth does this by working predominantly at parish level, helping to determine and address local needs and to design social action projects which respond to these needs, especially to help the most vulnerable. All the projects promoted will be firmly rooted in Catholic Social Teaching.

Go to **www.portsmouthdiocese.org.uk/caritas** to donate or for further information.

Appendix 3 - Prayerful Findings

These gems (the pilgrim blessing, prayer, beatitudes and reflection) were uncovered along the Way. They provided sources of entrustment and nourishment for my Camino days. Please take and use them on your Camino journey.

Pilgrim Blessing

from Burgos (days 11 & 12) at the Cathedral de Burgos and Capilla de la Divina Pastora

Almighty God, you always show mercy toward those who love you and you are never far away for those who seek you. Remain with your servants on this holy pilgrimage to Compostela and guide their way in accord with your will. Shelter them with your protection by day, give them the light of your grace by night, and, as their companion on the journey, bring them before the tomb of the apostle James in safety so they can experience your peace and your hope.

We ask this through Christ Our Lord. Amen.

The Pilgrim's Prayer

from Pamplona (day 4) at the Parish of San Cernin (Patron Saint of Pamplona)

Lord, you who called your servant Abraham out of the town of Ur in Chaldea and who watched over him during all his wanderings; you who guided the Jewish people through the desert; we ask you to watch over us, your servants, who for love of your name, make this pilgrimage to Santiago de Compostela.

Be for us,

> the companion on our journey,
> the guide at our crossroads,
> our strength in fatigue,
> our fortress in danger,
> our place of rest on the way,
> our shelter from the heat,
> our light in the darkness,
> our consolation in discouragement
> and the perseverance of our intention.

So that we under your guidance, safely and unhurt, may reach the end of our journey and strengthened with grace and virtue, secure and filled with happiness, may return to our home. Through Jesus Christ, Our Lord, Amen.

Apostle Saint James, pray for us

Holy Virgin Mary of the Way, pray for us

The Beatitudes of the Pilgrim

from Zabaldika

1. Blessed are you pilgrim, if you discover that the "camino" opens your eyes to what is not seen.

2. Blessed are you pilgrim, if what concerns you most is not to arrive, as to arrive with others.

3. Blessed are you pilgrim, when you contemplate the "camino" and you discover it is full of names and dawns.

4. Blessed are you pilgrim, because you have discovered that the authentic "camino" begins when it is completed.

5. Blessed are you pilgrim, if your knapsack is emptying of things and your heart does not know where to hang up so many feelings and emotions.

6. Blessed are you pilgrim, if you discover that one step back to help another is more valuable than a hundred forward without seeing what is at your side.

7. Blessed are you pilgrim, when you don't have words to give thanks for everything that surprises you at every twist and turn of the way.

8. Blessed are you pilgrim, if you search for the truth and make of the "camino" a life and of your life a "way", in search of the one who is the Way, the Truth and the Life.

9. Blessed are you pilgrim, if on the way you meet yourself and gift yourself with time, without rushing, so as not to disregard the image in your heart.

10. Blessed are you pilgrim, if you discover that the "camino" holds a lot of silence; and the silence of prayer; and the prayer of meeting with the Father who is waiting for you.

A reflection "Be still and know that I am God" (Psalm 46: 30)

on arrival from the Sisters Faithful Companions of Jesus (www.fcsisters.org)

- Allow some favourite moments of the Camino to come back to mind and realise that they are all blessings from God.
- Remember the needs of the world and all who need your love and your prayer.
- Thank God for the gifts you have received along the way and in your life.
- Place any other intentions you carry into the loving heart of God.

About the Author

David Sinclair is a family man with a wife and two grown-up children.

At the age of 24, he took a 7-month sabbatical from his work as a Consultant for a software application package to travel around the world. These travels paved the way to meeting his beautiful Filipino wife in 1995. His parents were not churchgoers, yet married life caused him to be beside his wife in church on Sundays. Something rubbed off! David was received into the Catholic Church in 2004, the year that he also ran the London Marathon. On fire with God's love, he currently serves in ministry as much as he can.

This is his first and, most likely, only book. He hopes that its offering has pleased Our Lord, who has steered him to this point to share the gift of his faith in this way. He may now restart his Diocesan led studies of the Word.

May Our Lord God bless this work and all the people it helps. Amen

"It is not the actual physical exertion that counts towards one's progress,

nor the nature of the task,

but by the spirit of faith with which it is undertaken."

St. Francis Xavier

Printed in Poland
by Amazon Fulfillment
Poland Sp. z o.o., Wrocław